evo
ASTON MARTIN

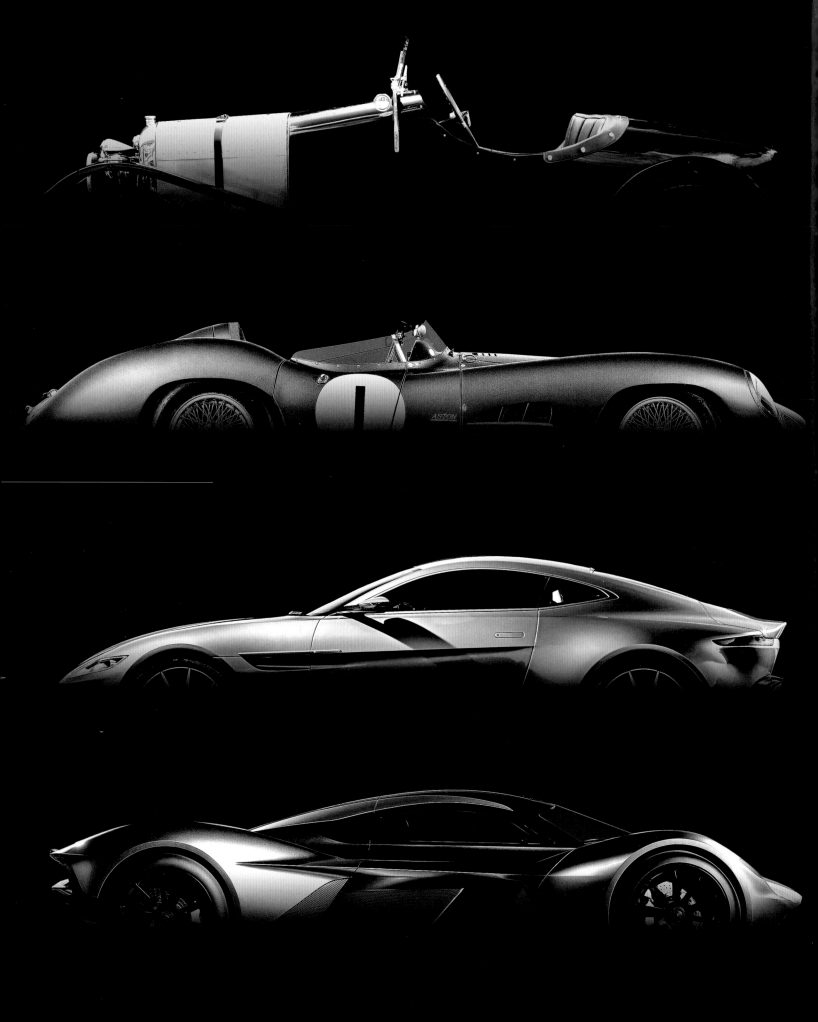

evo

ASTON MARTIN

BEHIND THE WHEEL OF A MOTORING ICON

ALL THE GREATEST ASTONS TRIED & TESTED

MITCHELL BEAZLEY

Contents

Recognized the world over, the iconic Aston Martin wings have graced some of the world's fastest, most stylish and most charismatic high-performance motorcars. From prewar racers to the classic DB models of the 1950s and 1960s to today's 200mph supercars, this is the story of those cars and what it feels like to drive them.

H ard to believe for such an iconic brand, but for most of its history Aston Martin teetered on the brink of insolvency. It was only the arrival of Ford in the late 1980s and the decision in the early '90s to adopt an abandoned Jaguar project and turn it into the hugely successful DB7 that finally made the marque profitable and assured it of a future. Until then it had been kept afloat by a succession of wealthy men (most were considerably less wealthy by the time they moved on) who were prepared to throw money at a small, idiosyncratic car maker with little hope of seeing a return on their investment.

Why did they do it? Probably for the same reasons that people have always loved Astons, the same reasons that you're holding this book – because there's a magical pull about the Aston Martin name and the cars that carry the famous wings.

Exactly what the words 'Aston Martin' evoke probably depends on your age. Those of more mature years recall the early DB models of the immediate postwar era, cars like the rakish DB2 and the fabulous DBR1 racer that famously won Le Mans in 1959. Those of us currently enjoying a midlife crisis go misty-eyed at the thought of the brutal V8 Vantage of the 1970s and 1980s. Younger fans download desktop wallpaper of Vanquishes and Vulcans. But everyone, of course, thinks of a certain DB5, painted in Silver Birch and kitted out with one or two items of non-standard equipment.

Ian Fleming had first paired James Bond with Aston Martin in the novel *Goldfinger*. In the book it was a DB MkIII, but by the time the film was made the DB5 was the latest model and so that was the one the producers wanted. It was to prove the perfect match for Sean Connery's 007:

both were the epitome of understated aggression and cool 1960s sophistication. Bond and Aston became cemented in the public consciousness, bywords for glamour and excitement, British icons recognized the world over.

The Bond connection certainly helped sell Astons and, for a time in the 1960s, the company books looked almost healthy. But even millionaire Sir David Brown couldn't make money from Aston Martin and in the early 1970s he bailed out. The company then entered its most turbulent period, as owners came and went and the famous factory at Newport Pagnell was even forced to close for a year. But through these difficult times, Aston somehow continued to attract brilliant – and highly resourceful – designers and engineers, and continued to make fabulous cars, like the V8 Vantage and the futuristic Lagonda.

Eventually came Ford money, the DB7, then, in 2000, Dr Ulrich Bez, the passionate German engineer who, as CEO, would drive the company to unprecedented levels of sales success with truly world-class products like the DB9 and the modern Vantage, without ever losing sight of what made Aston unique: that subtle blend of beauty, understated aggression, sizzling performance and a distinctively British character. And now Aston Martin has a new visionary at the helm, the personable and dynamic Englishman Andy Palmer, whose plans for the company outstrip anything we've yet seen. With new investors and a partnership with Mercedes-AMG to supply engines and electronic systems, a fresh generation of Astons is set to carry those famous wings to new heights.

THE EARLY YEARS

The Early Years – Introduction

From a crude horseless carriage called The Hybrid to some of the finest drivers' cars of the prewar era

T he earliest Aston Martins aren't just from a different age – they might as well be from a different universe, so far removed are they from today's ground-hugging supercars. Or so you might think. In fact these skinny-wheeled machines with their strange, boat-like bodies have a surprising amount in common with today's cars. Right from the start, Aston Martins were sporting machines with a strong English flavour, hand-built in small numbers for wealthy and discerning petrolheads.

It was on 15 January 1913 that Old Etonian Lionel Martin and his cycling friend Robert Bamford officially formed Bamford & Martin Ltd 'to deal in, manufacture and sell motor cars'. Based in Henniker Mews, in London's Kensington, they started out selling and tuning Singer cars. But Martin, in particular, was fired with an ambition to create his own machine, a 'British-built fast touring car… built up to the high ideals demanded by a small but extremely discriminating class of motorist'. The following year he tested a 1,389cc four-cylinder engine, built for him by Coventry-Simplex, in a 1908 Isotta Fraschini chassis – a car nicknamed The Hybrid. Subsequent success in the Aston Hill Climb inspired Lionel to coin the name Aston Martin for his proposed marque.

The first car to be actually registered as an Aston Martin came a year later, in March 1915, and was nicknamed –

Founders Lionel Martin (left) and Robert Bamford

Martin at Brooklands in 1921 with an early car known as Bunny

rather unflatteringly – Coal Scuttle because of the shape of its bodywork. Alas, events in Europe would soon put all such trivial activities on hold. It wasn't until 1919 that Lionel Martin could reassemble his small team (Bamford by now fading from the picture) and take up where they'd left off.

The next few cars, with names like Buzzbox, Razor Blade and Bunny, were also one-offs. Another, more prosaically known as A3, is today the oldest surviving Aston Martin. In 1923 it lapped the Brooklands circuit, with its banked turns, at a surely terrifying 84.5mph.

Lionel Martin often raced these cars himself to prove their mettle. Another driver of these early Astons was the rich playboy Count Louis Zborowski, who liked them so much that in 1922 he invested £10,270/$41,080 in the company, a colossal sum in those days. Sadly, the count was to die at the wheel of a Mercedes at Monza two years later.

Other investors followed. Aston Martin was always struggling for money in those early days, but in 1923 it began offering its latest model – the Sports – to the general public for the first time, and the following year sales hit a peak of 26 cars. It was a false dawn. In 1925 the company was placed in receivership and Lionel Martin left amid bitter recriminations.

The next chapter began in October 1926 with the formation of a new company, Aston Martin Motors, run by

engineer and racer Augustus Cesare 'Bert' Bertelli and William Renwick, with a new works in a former aircraft factory in Feltham, Middlesex. The heart of the new Aston Martins was a 1.5-litre OHC engine, which would go on to power a whole generation of not only sports and racing cars, but also saloons and tourers.

It was these 'Bertelli Astons' that really established Aston Martin as a marque to be reckoned with. Despite money problems never being far away and several changes of backers, the cars enjoyed many successes in competition, not only at Brooklands, but also at Le Mans, where they scored a number of class wins.

Aston Martin naturally used this racing glory to sell its sports cars, with models like the LM (for Le Mans) and the Ulster (named to celebrate a team victory in the Ulster Tourist Trophy race) proving especially popular with the young dashers of the heady interwar years.

These 1930s Astons were real drivers' cars, their combination of strong performance, excellent handling, stylish lines, fine engineering and quality of construction making them highly prized by the rich young men who could afford them. They established Aston Martin among the world's most desirable and valuable sporting machines, and by 1937 the company was producing 140 cars a year.

The 1934 Le Mans squad about to leave Feltham and head for France

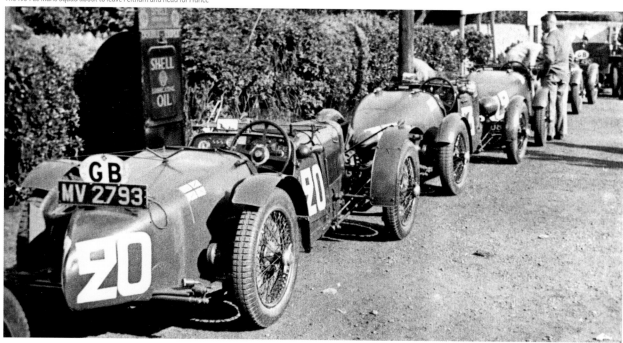

DESIGNED
& BUILT
FOR THE
YEARS

"LE MANS"
2/4 SEATER
SPORTS MODEL

This model is the direct outcome of our extensive road racing experience and outstanding competition successes at Le Mans and elsewhere. It is a true racing car, with a tip-top road performance, adapted for general sporting purposes, and not a touring or roadster car outwardly transformed by racing gadgets. The body provides comfortable seating for two, with convenient luggage, or additional passenger accommodation. It is economical to a degree and perhaps its most outstanding feature is that it maintains its "tune" and faultless performance without constant adjustment. Under really hard driving, 26 to 27 m.p.g. of petrol and a correspondingly good oil consumption is obtained.

LE MANS MODEL
2/4 seater (8 ft. 6 in. chassis)   £595
85/90 m.p.h.

ASTON-MARTIN
A PRODUCT OF BRITISH CRAFTSMANSHIP

ENGINE SPECIFICATION

The underlying aim in the design of this is reliability and durability at high speeds, and the ability to "hold its tune" without constant attention, hence the dry sump lubrication system, unusual valve gear, and special camshaft drive.

ENGINE 4 cylinders, bore 69 mm., stroke 99 mm., 1493 c.c. R.A.C. rating 11.9 h.p. Tax £12 max. b.h.p. 70 @ 4750 r.p.m. Compression ratio 7.5/1.

CAMSHAFT AND VALVE GEAR The camshaft is mounted in an aluminium casting, and is supported by three large diameter plain bearings. It is driven by a chain at the front end of the engine, and a feature of this drive is that the chain itself is driven from a countershaft running at half engine speed, instead of direct from the crankshaft. This ensures that the chain speed is relatively low even at high engine r.p.m.

An arrangement is provided so that the cylinder head, camshaft and valve gear may be removed without dismantling the chain and losing the valve timing.

The chain itself is kept permanently in adjustment by a Weller spring directly placed in the main oil return from the overhead gear.

LUBRICATION Two oil pumps enclosed in a common housing bolted on to the front of the engine are driven direct from the countershaft. One pump is 50% larger than the other and acts as a scavenger, drawing warm oil from the sump and returning it to the oil tank between the front dumb irons. The other pump forces cool oil from the tank to the engine by way of a close grained pressure filter running its whole length. From this the oil is pressure fed to main bearings, big ends and overhead gear. The capacity of the oil tank is 2½ gallons.

COOLING A combination of thermo syphon and pump cooling is used. The cylinder walls are cooled by the usual thermo syphon arrangement and a water pump driven by a dog on the front of the timing gear forces a stream of cooling water directly through the cylinder head, thus ensuring that there are no "hot spots" when the engine is kept "flat out" for any length of time.

CYLINDERS AND CRANK CASE The cylinders and crank case are cast in one, so producing a block of great rigidity.

CRANKSHAFT The crankshaft is made of Nitralloy and is very stiff, carefully balanced, and carried in three large white metal bearings, and thus able to run at high r.p.m. without vibration.

PISTONS AND CONNECTING RODS Duralumin connecting rods are used in conjunction with aluminium pistons to ensure good heat dissipation and extreme lightness.

* A unique feature of the ASTON-MARTIN Engine is the DRY SUMP LUBRICATION. From the 2½ gal. cooling tank between the front dumb irons oil is constantly pumped through the engine (via extra large oil ducts) and returned for cooling at the rate of 2 gals. per minute at 3,000 r.p.m. Consequently the oil temperature cannot rise above 75° C. even under racing conditions and bearing failure is a practical impossibility.

The absence of a deep sump facilitates very low engine mounting and vastly increases the stability of the car.

ASTON-MARTIN
Yours for all time
Telephone: 218
ASTON-MARTIN LTD. FELTHAM MIDDLESEX

"LE MANS"
Special
4-Seater

"Long distance road racing is our experimental department"

A further development of the Le Mans type is this SPECIAL Long Chassis Model. It has been evolved to provide a Sports Car of similar performance, with accommodation for four people.

The lengthened chassis, in addition to providing adequate additional seating, permits of still more sweeping and graceful body lines. The specification in general is that of the two seater model, although certain variations of equipment have been made to meet general requirements. For instance, the windscreen has two detachable side wings. When the main screen is folded flat over the bonnet, these two wings may be detached from the sides and fixed in position to form small individual screens, for driver and passenger.

4 SEATER "SPECIAL"
(10 ft. chassis) 80/85 m.p.h.   £625

ASTON-MARTIN
A PRODUCT OF BRITISH CRAFTSMANSHIP

But it wasn't enough for the marque's backers to see a return on their investment. 'Bert' Bertelli fell out with the moneymen and left, and, as the storm clouds gathered over Europe once again, production fell to a mere half-dozen cars by 1939.

With the outbreak of war, production was suspended and the factory forced to survive on military contracts. There was a glimmer of hope, though. In March 1939, the company unveiled its 'car of the future', an odd-looking but undeniably advanced machine designed by chief engineer Claude Hill and christened Atom. The Aston Martin story was about to take its most significant twist.

Ahead of its time: Atom of 1939 was Aston's 'car of the future'

1921

A3

Originally built in 1921, then rediscovered and restored 80 years later, A3 is the oldest surviving Aston Martin

This car is the tangible link with the early days of Aston Martin, when Bamford and Martin were building their first cars in a workshop in Kensington, and Lionel Martin himself was racing and hill-climbing them at venues across the south of England. The very first, which subsequently became known as Coal Scuttle, racked up 15,000 competitive miles. Then, in 1920, the company built its second car, powered by a new four-cylinder engine designed by ex-Coventry-Simplex man H V Robb, with competition in mind, and its beefed-up chassis was used in the next three prototypes.

A3 was the third Aston Martin built, and is the oldest survivor today. First registered as AM273 and initially bearing the chassis number 'No.3', it appeared in 1921 and covered many 'development' miles, mostly at Brooklands. Depending on the event, it might be powered by the single-overhead-camshaft engine or a later twin-cam, or a racing version of the earlier side-valve engine. The mix-and-match nature of A3 didn't finish there. Two bodies were used during this period: a streamlined racing style and a more conventional sports item.

Retired from development duties after two years and sold to its first private owner, Captain J C Douglas, the car was given a new engine and had its chassis renumbered to match.

It was also re-registered XN2902 and even susbsequently rebodied in the 1930s. All of which, of course, caused some confusion for later historians!

However, when the car resurfaced at auction in 2002, experts from the Aston Martin Heritage Trust recognized its significance, raised the funds to buy it and commissioned a full restoration, taking it back to the two-seater sports configuration it was originally when sold to Captain Douglas.

What really stops you dead in your tracks when you see A3 for the first time is just how small and perfectly proportioned it is. Climbing into the snug cockpit, you find a wonderful legs-outstretched driving position, perfect for competition. Typically for a racer of this era, the pedal layout is alien to those brought up on more modern cars: the centre-mounted throttle is on the left-hand side of the steering column and takes some time to get used to.

Firing up the side-valve engine with its button is simple enough, once the fuel system is primed, and little effort is needed to make it burst into life. Most impressively, it quickly settles down into a smooth, even and quiet idle. On the move, the steering is light and accurate, and the acceleration surprisingly brisk. It's a proper, sporting machine but, given its origins, that should come as no surprise.

SPECIFICATIONS

Years produced: 1921 **Engine:** In-line 4-cylinder, 1,389cc **Max power:** c.50bhp
Max torque: n/a **0–60mph:** n/a
Max speed: c.85mph **Price:** £1 million+/$1.24 million today

1929
LM3

LM3 is a fine example of an early Bertelli-era Aston and was even raced by 'Bert' Bertelli himself

SPECIFICATIONS

Years produced: 1929 **Engine:** In-line 4-cylinder, 1,488cc **Max power:** c.65bhp originally (c.100bhp today)
Max torque: n/a **0–60mph:** n/a
Max speed: 100mph+ **Price:** £1 million+/$1.24 million today

O ne of a series of cars built to race at Le Mans (although this particular car never actually did), LM3 shows just how far Aston Martins had come by the late 1920s. The marque had already been through the first of many changes of ownership, and the cars of this period were very much the vision of new co-owner and chief engineer Augustus Cesare 'Bert' Bertelli. Bertelli himself sat in this very cockpit for LM3's competition debut at the 1929 Brooklands Double Twelve. He and 'riding mechanic' Jack Bezzant finished fifth in that race, and the same pairing achieved ninth place in the 1929 Irish Grand Prix. Later successes for LM3 would include victory in a five-lap handicap race at Donington in 1935 in the hands of another famous figure in Aston circles: racing driver and owners' club co-founder St John Horsfall. So it's positively dripping with period history.

Sat in the upright seat and gripping the cord-bound steering wheel, the driver first has to reprogram his brain to the centre throttle, with its AM-embossed brass pedal-pad like those of its neighbours. At least the gearbox has a conventional gate pattern, not reversed like that of a later Le Mans model. With practice you can get mostly crunch-free upshifts; a double-declutch with a well-timed blip is obligatory for the downshifts. The size of that blip is absolutely critical when selecting second from third; this is not a forgiving gearbox.

The steering feels a lot more precise than the spindly linkage and springy steering wheel suggest. It's light and smooth, complementing a ride of surprising suppleness. There's a little bit of scuttle-shudder over bumps but the abiding impression is of a surprisingly all-of-a-piece machine.

So pretty soon you're enjoying the noisy enthusiasm of the 1,488cc, four-cylinder engine with its overhead camshaft and crossflow cylinder head. It gives more power now than it did when new and zooms easily to an indicated 70mph on the small speedometer and 4,000rpm on the outsize rev-counter.

In corners, the front wheels are pushed a little wide if you go gently into a bend, but a dab of the middle pedal quickly quells that and brings on a pleasing tail-drift with which you can fine-tune your cornering line.

It's as old-school rear-drive as you can get, and if it's all happening too quickly, there are strong, progressive brakes to rein in the pace. LM3, then, is a delightful machine and one that wears its history with pride.

SPECIFICATIONS

Years produced: 1934 **Engine:** In-line 4-cylinder, 1,495cc **Max power:** c.100bhp @ 5,500rpm
Max torque: n/a **0–60mph:** n/a
Max speed: 100mph+ **Price:** £3 million+/$3.7 million today

1934

LM15

The greatest of all prewar Aston models – on both road and track – was the Ulster, and LM15 is one of the best examples of this revered breed

Strictly speaking, **LM15** predated the Ulster model. It was one of three factory team cars entered for the 1934 Tourist Trophy race, which in those days was run on a closed-road circuit in Northern Ireland. All three finished the gruelling race, winning the team prize for Aston Martin. In their honour, customer versions of the car would thereafter be known as the Ulster. So, to nitpick, LM15 is only retrospectively an Ulster. It doesn't matter. All feature the same, spirited 1.5-litre overhead-cam four-cylinder engine, the long, louvred bonnet, the cycle wings and the distinctive tail (which actually housed the spare wheel). And all are an absolute joy to drive. Once sunk into the leather bucket seat, you're immediately struck by just how close everything is to the driver: the large steering wheel, the dashboard, the screen, the wheels and, indeed, the surface of the track.

The 1,495cc engine springs into life easily, sounding bigger than it is. This is the first level of car-driver communication to reach you, since the engine is solidly mounted on the chassis. This means that the driver can feel a lot of the engine's behaviour as well as hear it – and feel its temperature, too. Winter motoring is entirely possible thanks to the vast amounts of engine heat coming through into the cockpit: it's like having a wood-burning stove in the car with you.

A dip of the light clutch, engage first (top right) and the Ulster comes truly to life. As you catch a waft of warm Castrol 'R', you can feel the entire car writhing around you. The scuttle is moving, and while the steering column stays rock-steady, the seat is telling you that the simple ladder chassis is as much a part of the handling package as the leaf springs and friction dampers. Forget chassis rigidity – that was hard to achieve in the 1930s, so the designers actively exploited the fact. There is not much suspension travel but the solid front and rear axles do not complain. Few modern cars can out-corner an Ulster.

Indeed, the Ulster is arguably the best-handling prewar car of them all. When raced against bigger-engined rivals, it's the handling that allows the Ulster to win through – specifically, its ability to carry speed through corners. It needs to, since c.100bhp cannot power the car out of corners as well as some. That said, four-wheel drifts are as natural as breathing in this car. Ulsters just do not bite and, if you take a liberty, it will tell you before you get into real trouble.

While you can get away with misbehaving a little, an Ulster rewards smoothness and commitment. Hesitate and you lose speed; brake too much or get it too sideways and speed is not easily regained. The steering is heavy, but you don't notice it once moving. For a worm-and-castor drop-link steering system setup, it offers surprising accuracy and feel. And placing the car on the track couldn't be easier, since the view of the front wheels is unimpeded. The cable-operated brakes, while heavy to operate, are powerful enough to outbrake rivals when racing. The straight-cut gearbox is easy to handle with the lever so close to the steering wheel, and the pedals, which are laid out with the throttle in the middle and the brake pedal to the right, are set high for perfect heel-and-toe action. Generally, third and fourth gears are all you need once on the move, though a hairpin may demand second. The shift, with decent double-declutching, is strong, direct and quick. Throttle pick-up through the twin SUs is instant and between 4,000 and 5,500rpm (the red line is at 6,000rpm). The power is strong and perfectly in tune with the rest of the car.

When LM15's sister car, LM20, came third overall at Le Mans in 1935, it did so on a rough track at an average speed of over 75mph, including pit stops. That was a staggering feat but, aside from the act of human endurance, it's easy to see how it was achieved in a car of such huge competence. And easy to understand why its drivers wore such broad smiles.

THE
DAVID BROWN
YEARS

The David Brown Years – Introduction

How a Yorkshire industrialist bought struggling Aston Martin for a mere £20,500/$82,000

and turned it into one of the world's greatest marques

Remember the Atom, the one-off prewar Aston prototype created by chief engineer Claude Hill? It may have been an odd-looking thing, but it was genuinely advanced for its day, with streamlined aluminium bodywork over a supporting steel tubular frame, coil-sprung front suspension, and a 2-litre four-cylinder overhead-valve engine of Hill's own design.

So, although it looked odd, it drove really well. Indeed, while Aston Martin survived the war on military contracts, company owner Gordon Sutherland clocked up an astonishing 100,000 miles in the Atom. And in 1947, when he ran out of cash and advertised the company for sale in *The Times*, it was a spin in the Atom that convinced northern industrialist David Brown to buy Aston Martin.

Brown (not yet Sir David) was at the time the boss of the David Brown group of companies, which raked in millions making tractors for agriculture and gears for industry. A keen sportsman and motorist, and also the possessor of a sizeable ego, he loved the idea of owning a sports-car company and going racing, and the Atom convinced him that Aston had the talent to make it happen.

There was only one problem: Brown couldn't see much potential in Hill's four-cylinder OHV engine. But he knew that similarly cash-strapped Lagonda had a 2.6-litre six-cylinder twin-cam engine that had been developed under W O Bentley. That was much more the ticket. So he bought Lagonda as well.

Development continued, and two years later Aston Martin entered three prototype versions of its sleek new DB2

Man with a mission: Yorkshireman David Brown

The first car to carry Brown's initials was the DB2 of 1949

models for the 1949 Le Mans race, two with the four-cylinder engine and one with the Lagonda six-cylinder. That car failed to finish, but one of the four-cylinder cars came seventh. The following year, Aston entered three six-cylinder DB2s. Two of them finished first and second in the 3-litre class and fifth and sixth overall. The same year, exports to America began. The DB era of Aston Martin was truly under way.

The next two decades would see a succession of world-class road cars. DB2 evolved into DB2/4 and 2/4 MkIII. Then came DB4, 5 and 6 with their gorgeous, Touring-designed bodies and glorious all-aluminium straight-six engines. By the time the 1964 release of *Goldfinger* saw James Bond behind the wheel of a DB5, Aston Martin was synonymous with glamour and excitement, helped to no small degree by

the fabulous DBR1 winning Le Mans outright in 1959. Aston Martin was now Britain's Ferrari, its new factory at Newport Pagnell in Buckinghamshire the equivalent of Maranello.

The final car of the David Brown era was the DBS, which appeared first with the straight-six and then, in 1969, with an all-new 5.3-litre V8 engine that re-established Aston Martin in the top flight of luxury, high-performance car makers.

Alas, while the cars were performing, the company wasn't. Aston Martin Lagonda had never made any serious money for Sir David (he'd been knighted in 1968) and by the early 1970s it was actually draining cash from other parts of the DB group. So, with heavy heart, he sold the company for a token £100/$240. It was a sad end to a glorious era, but what magnificent machines he left us.

ASTON MARTIN

THE DAVID BROWN ASTON MARTIN DB4

2-Litre Sports (DB1)

The first road car of the David Brown era was a classy machine, but it barely hinted at what was to come

David Brown was hardly one to shy away from an opportunity to push the 'DB' brand, which makes it all the more surprising that the first model launched under his ownership of Aston Martin didn't wear the famous initials. It was only several years later, after the launch of the DB2, that the 2-Litre Sports became known retrospectively as DB1.

But then in many ways the DB1 didn't really fit the template for what we now regard as a classic DB Aston. Its rolling curves were not without appeal, but they lacked the taut, low-slung, long-bonneted sporting mien of the cars that followed. It wasn't particularly dashing to drive, either, its 2-litre four producing a modest 90bhp and struggling to propel the rather portly body past 90mph. And this at a time when Jaguar's sleek new XK roadster had recently topped 120mph.

In other ways, though, the DB1 did set the mould. It was an expensive, hand-built machine with a high-quality feel and more than a dash of glamour. Its distinctive three-piece grille would be carried over to the DB2 and would eventually

morph (via the DB MkIII) into the DB4's signature aperture. While it wasn't quick, it rode and handled well. And, like many subsequent Astons, it was built in tiny numbers – in fact just 15 were eventually completed, which makes it one of the rarest and most collectible of all. When a 'barn-find' example in need of total restoration came on the market in 2013, it was snapped up for a cool £100,000/$155,000.

Under the skin, the DB1 was a development of the prewar Aston prototype called the Atom, whose excellent road manners had so impressed David Brown. When Brown took control of the company in 1947, work began immediately on a drophead coupé based on the Atom platform and 2-litre four-cylinder overhead-valve engine but with new Frank Feeley bodywork, coil springs instead of leaves at the rear, and a David Brown gearbox. Thus the 2-litre Sports was born, making its debut at the 1948 Earls Court motor show.

Owners today are rather fond of their DB1s. Outright performance is no longer an issue, and they can enjoy the car's pleasing character, engaging dynamics and not least the significant part it played in the Aston Martin story.

SPECIFICATIONS

Years produced: 1948–50 **Engine:** In-line 4-cylinder, 1,970cc **Max power:** 90bhp
Max torque: n/a **0–60mph:** n/a **Max speed:** 93mph
Price: £2,332/$11,357 new in 1948, c.£350,000+/$435,650+ today

1950
DB2

The DB2 – and its DB2/4 four-seater offspring – set the template for generations of Astons to follow

SPECIFICATIONS

Years produced: 1950–57 (DB2 and 2/4)
Engine: In-line 6-cylinder, 2,922cc (DB2/4 MkII) **Max power:** c.140bhp @ 5,000rpm
Max torque: n/a **0–60mph:** 10.5sec **Max speed:** 120mph
Price: £2,621/$6,295 new in 1954, c.£150,000–£250,000/$186,500–$311,150 today

T he Frank Feeley-styled DB2, launched in April 1950, was the first to carry David Brown's initials. It also created the basic template for practically every Aston that has followed: a powerful, large-capacity front-mounted engine under a rakishly long bonnet; sleek fastback bodywork with the option of a drophead version; a well-appointed cabin; and, of course, excellent road manners.

What is sometimes forgotten is that the DB2 had a pretty handy competition record, too. When three cars were entered for the 1950 Le Mans, two of them finished first and second in the 3-litre class, and fifth and sixth overall. The following year, another three-car entry went even better, claiming third, fifth and seventh overall, and taking the first three places in class.

The DB2, then, was every inch a sporting car, and the road testers of the day were in raptures about the new Aston Martin. The staff of *The Autocar* racked up 1,900 miles in ten days, describing the engine (initially 2.6 litres) as 'one of the finest in existence' and lavishing praise on the DB2's high-speed stability.

The DB2/4 arrived in 1953, with two occasional rear seats added (hence the '4'), which could be folded forwards to create a useful load area, one that could be accessed via the 2/4's handy top-hinged tailgate – an innovation that gave the Aston reasonable claim to being the world's first 'hatchback'.

Engine capacity grew to 2.9 litres in 1954, peak power climbing to 140bhp, dropping the 0–60 time to 10.5 seconds and lifting the maximum to a nice round 120mph. For those wanting even more, Aston offered a Special Series engine with larger valves, higher-lift camshafts and a quoted 165bhp.

In 1955 came the MkII version with detail improvements, and the same year the range was expanded to include a hard-top coupé version of the drophead. Just 34 of these 'notchback' models were built and they're particularly sought-after today.

To drive them, they feel very much of their time, the steering and brakes in particular being hard work unless they've been subtly upgraded, but they're cars of strong heart and rich character, and, when you take them by the scruff of the neck, their sporting pedigree shines through.

SPECIFICATIONS

Years produced: 1953–56 **Engine:** In-line 6-cylinder, 2,922cc **Max power:** 217bhp @ 6,000rpm
Max torque: n/a **0–60mph:** 6.0sec (est)
Max speed: 150mph (est) **Price:** c.£5 million+/$6.2 million today

DB3S

The first car to feature the iconic Aston grille, the DB3S was a superbly effective race car –
and a stunningly beautiful one, too

T he DB3S comes from a time when racing cars could be effective yet still beautiful, and this was designer Frank Feeley's masterpiece. Aesthetically stunning but with reason, not just good taste. So, the cutaway front arches are there to remove heat from the radiator and front brakes. The 'Cathedral arch' ridges, which run the length of the wings and bonnet, add strength to the body as well as accentuating its sensuous lines. The sublime grille opening – whose shape is evident in every subsequent Aston Martin to this day – cleverly divides and directs air to where it's needed.

In the 3-litre class of the day, DB3Ss were nearly always the cars to beat – and on tracks with shorter straights than Le Mans they would often show the bigger-engined D-types and Ferraris a clean pair of heels, too. Not that their record at Le Mans was too shabby, finishing second overall in both 1955 and 1956.

Approaching the car, one is struck by how small it is, and its petite, feline grace. The simplicity of the exterior conceals some sophisticated underpinnings – not just the chassis, but also the David Brown gearbox, which was developed for the 1955 cars with innovative needle roller bearings. The engine is the ultimate development of the LB6 unit that Brown acquired

when he bought Lagonda, with twin spark plugs per cylinder, Weber carburettors and magnesium castings.

What the DB3S lacked in outright speed compared with the larger-engined Jaguars and Ferraris of the time, it made up for with a chassis that was wonderfully communicative and beautifully balanced.

Heading out onto a track, you're struck again by its compactness and, as the speed rises, by the controlled suppleness of the chassis. Though body-roll is minimal, suspension travel is much greater than on many modern road cars. So it soaks up undulations, without in any way feeling soggy. In fact it feels deliciously taut.

However hard you drive, you get a feeling of togetherness and a sense that the car is looking after you. The steering, neither particularly heavy in the paddock nor over-light on the track, is just perfectly balanced, its responses precise, the feedback immense.

It's just as well that the chassis is so benign because this is a properly fast machine. The pull through the rev-range to 6,000rpm is wonderfully strong, while steering on the throttle is easy and not the mad scrabble that, say, a D-type can entail. No wonder the racers of the day loved the DB3S.

1955
DB3S Coupé

Originally conceived as a Le Mans racer, then revamped as a road car,

the coupé version of the DB3S is one of the rarest of all Astons

SPECIFICATIONS

Years produced: 1955–56 **Engine:** In-line 6-cylinder, 2,922cc **Max power:** 211bhp @ 5,500rpm
Max torque: 222lb ft @ 4,500rpm **0–60mph:** 6.6sec **Max speed:** 140mph
Price: £4,810/$13,468 new in 1955, £5 million+/$6.2 million+ today

T he concept was sound enough: the open DB3S was a great car but to go even faster, such as at Le Mans, needed more aerodynamic bodywork, so a coupé version was built. Sure enough it was quicker, but it was also less stable at high speed. This was manifest at the 1954 Le Mans, when both entries suffered rear-end lift, crashing at virtually the same spot.

None of this stood in the way of a production DB3S Coupé becoming available at the 1955 Earls Court motor show. It was now fully trimmed and with a smaller fuel tank, allowing a decent-sized luggage area behind the seats. But it was fiercely expensive, too, and rather extreme for most drivers. Just three were produced before all DB3S production ceased the following year.

Driving one today is a privilege. It is compact and cosy, with limited headroom for over six-footers in the narrow cockpit, while the interior, unlike in more rudimentary racers, is beautifully trimmed. Once warm, the straight-six pulls strongly from 2,000rpm and will spin eagerly to 5,500 and its 211bhp peak output and beyond. Back in the day, *Autosport* recorded an impressive 0–60mph time of 6.6 seconds and a 140mph maximum. Throttle response is instantaneous as the triple Webers snort air, accompanied by a glorious snarl from the twin exhaust pipes exiting just below the driver's door.

The perfectly placed short-throw lever for the David Brown gearbox is satisfyingly light and precise in engagement, and the ride is surprisingly supple, but not at the expense of roadholding. Turn-in is precise, and feedback through the sensitive, high-geared steering is excellent, the handling as beautifully balanced as the contours of the coachwork. The DB3S Coupé may have been a cul-de-sac for Aston Martin, but what an exquisite one!

34

1957
DB2/4 MkIII

Taking the grille from the DB3S and with a host of refinements, this was the ultimate incarnation

of the Feltham Aston

SPECIFICATIONS

Years produced: 1957–59 **Engine:** In-line six-cylinder, 2,922cc **Max power:** 162bhp @ 5,500rpm
Max torque: 180lb ft @ 4,000rpm **0–60mph:** 9.3sec **Max speed:** c.120mph
Price: £3,076/$6,995 (saloon) new in 1957, £150,000–£250,000/$186,700–$311,150 (saloon) today

hat a difference a grille makes... The earlier DB2 and 2/4 always had good proportions, but their rather rudimentary grilles did look as though they'd been bashed out by the local blacksmith. For the MkIII, launched in 1957, stylist Frank Feeley adopted the sculpted aperture that he'd designed for the DB3S racer, and it was just what the road car needed. No more dodgy British dentistry; the Aston mouth was now a perfect blend of beauty and aggression.

That same signature shape was echoed inside with the new instrument binnacle, which finally placed all the dials directly in front of the driver, and there were bucket seats in place of the previous benches.

The Willie Watson-designed LB6 straight-six had already grown from 2.6 to 2.9 litres in 1954, and now it was further developed for the MkIII, making it both stronger and more powerful. Peak power in standard tune on twin SUs was quoted as 162bhp at 5,500rpm, with the option of a 180bhp triple-carb Special Series engine. The MkIII also saw the standard fitment of front disc brakes.

The MkIII brought the DB2/4 up to date and it stayed in production well into 1959, overlapping with the DB4. There were drophead and fixed-head coupé versions, but the majority of the 550-odd built were saloons, or, rather, hatchbacks.

The driver's door is surprisingly small and light, clicking shut with a gentle touch and satisfying precision. The sill and floor are high, so threading yourself under the large steering wheel requires a bit of thought and contortion, but, once into the bucket seat, the comfort and ergonomics are excellent.

As standard, Feltham Astons are heavy to drive, so many owners now add electric power steering, which is a real boon: while lessening the load, it does nothing to remove 'feel'. Acceleration is strong and must have felt incredible in its day. At around 4,500rpm, you can sense the power curve flattening out while the straight-six begins to rumble in mild protest, but the pace that the engine can generate is very impressive. The gearbox, a David Brown unit, is a delight, while the brake pedal has fabulous feedback, and the pedals are well placed for heeling-and-toeing. All in all, as a more affordable alternative to a DB4, the MkIII has a lot going for it.

SPECIFICATIONS

Years produced: 1957–59
Engine: In-line six-cylinder, 2,992cc **Max power:** c.260bhp @ 6,250rpm
Max torque: n/a **0–60mph:** c.5sec (est)
Max speed: c.160mph **Price:** £20 million+/$24.9 million+ today

DBR1

This was the car with which David Brown finally fulfilled his dream of winning Le Mans outright

DB2s and DB3Ss had scored class wins at Le Mans, but no Aston Martin had ever won the 24 Hours outright, and it took until 1959 before the stars finally aligned and David Brown had the victory he'd been seeking ever since he took control of Aston Martin 12 years earlier. And when a DBR1 won the TT race at Goodwood later that summer, Aston Martin also secured the World Sportscar Championship. David Brown had his victory at last.

Crucially, it was a change in the sports-car racing regulations, moving away from production-based cars, that allowed the team – led by engineer Ted Cutting – to create the DBR1 from a clean sheet of paper. Although visually related to the DB3S, the new car was a far more exotic concoction, with a multi-tubular spaceframe under the wafer-thin 20-gauge aluminium bodywork, and de Dion rear suspension with a rear-mounted transaxle gearbox, while the highly tuned dry-sump twin-plug RB6 engine was specially developed for the DBR1, first in 2.5-litre form and later 3-litre.

Only five were ever built and they're the most highly coveted Astons: the 1959 Le Mans-winning car itself changed hands for around £20 million/$25 million a few years ago.

Driving such a car is, of course, a special honour. Wriggle down as far as you can in the small bucket seat, press the starter and hear the electrical whirr then the musical bark, followed by the searing crackle as you back off, that only six cylinders arranged in-line can make. Reach down for the stumpy gear lever, select first in the conventional H-pattern gate, and away. The clutch is smooth, and the gears – once the oil circulating from the tank has warmed a little – engage easily enough. The faster you throw the lever, the less effort it takes and the smoother the shift. The engine is smooth and sweet but needs to be kept between 5000 and 6800rpm for it to work best. Kept there, it brays and wails, sounding as 'revvy' as it is.

The response to the wheel is instant, and almost immediately the Aston adopts a slightly oversteering stance, yawing its tail about five or ten degrees to the side. Hold that yaw with a dose of power, tickling it more and more through the corner until your foot is flat to the floor by the exit. When it does finally sling its tail, you need a big dose of opposite lock – and for that you need a well-braced torso and strong arms.

The DBR1 did what it was built to do – capturing the World Championship and Le Mans – and in incomparable style.

1958
DB4

A landmark car for Aston Martin, the DB4 caused a sensation in 1958

and still gets enthusiasts' hearts racing today

SPECIFICATIONS

Years produced: 1958–63 **Engine:** In-line six-cylinder, 3,670cc **Max power:** 240bhp @ 5,500rpm
Max torque: 240lb ft @ 4,250rpm **0–60mph:** 8.5sec **Max speed:** 140mph
Price: £3,980/$7,475 new in 1962, £500,000+/$622,350+ today

When the DB4 was unveiled in October 1958, Aston Martin vaulted effortlessly into the top flight of the world's most prestigious marques. Here was a thoroughly modern, high-performance GT car every bit as desirable and capable as any contemporary Ferrari. *Autosport* magazine described it as the 'safest and fastest in the world'.

The styling was the work of Italian design house Touring, and the DB4 used that company's patented *superleggera* (super-light) construction method: a lattice of small-diameter steel tubes clothed in aluminium panels, all supported by engineer Harold Beach's platform chassis.

Engine designer Tadek Marek's all-new, all-aluminium, double-overhead-cam straight-six, another defining element of the Aston Martin story, also arrived with the DB4. In standard tune it made a claimed 240bhp at 5,500rpm, enough for a top speed of 140mph. A four-speed David Brown gearbox, rack-and-pinion steering and servo-assisted Dunlop disc brakes for all four wheels completed the mechanical package.

Triple-carburettor Vantage versions add an extra dash of excitement, but even in standard twin-SU form the DB4 is quick enough for today's traffic. The DB gearbox requires a patient and sensitive hand if you're only used to modern gearboxes, but once everything's warmed through and you've adapted to its natural tempo, it can be palmed around with satisfying ease.

Give the straight-six its head in third gear from a little above jogging pace to somewhere on the naughty side of the legal limit, and acceleration swells in a most agreeable fashion, the guttural exhaust and induction roar compressing and hardening as the revs pass 4,000rpm. It's the sound of a thoroughbred British performance car. The brakes, too, are adequate for regular road driving – push through the initial deadness and there's solid stopping power.

Many owners have power-assisted steering retro-fitted. As standard, the steering's low gearing means you have to grab big armfuls of lock in tight turns, but there is another way: if

there's room to play, the DB4 is more than happy to steer on the throttle.

What makes the DB4 such a special and important car is the way it fixed the template so perfectly for everything we still enjoy today about Aston's best road cars: that combination of transcendently handsome but unshowy good looks, abundant and unaffected performance, well-balanced chassis, and rich and arguably unique character. A brilliant amalgam of Latin-infused style and lion-hearted British engineering, it deserves its lofty position in the ranks of great Aston Martins.

SPECIFICATIONS

Years produced: 1959–63 **Engine:** In-line straight-six, 3,670cc **Max power:** 302bhp @ 6,000rpm
Max torque: 240lb ft @ 5,000rpm **0–60mph:** 6.1sec **Max speed:** 153mph
Price: £4,668/$8,700 new, £2.5 million+/$3.1 million+ today

1959
DB4 GT

Take the DB4, shorten the wheelbase, shed some weight and add more power.
Result: one of the most intoxicating Astons of all

S o the DB4 was already a game-changer for Aston Martin. As a road car it could stand toe to toe with the greatest of the era. But it wasn't a racing car, and racing was deep in the blood of Aston in the late 1950s. So the DB4 became the starting point for a more extreme machine. At the Paris show in 1959 – exactly a year after the DB4's own launch – Aston officially unveiled the GT, the perfect car for the wealthy 'gentlemen racers' of the day.

Just under 13cm (5in) had been cut from the wheelbase to improve the handling. The rear seats had been dispensed with and a huge 30-gallon fuel tank was now fitted in the tail. The glass in the side and rear windows was replaced with Perspex, and the headlights were now under streamlined covers, providing a glimpse of how the DB5 would look a few years later.

The changes went further still. The brakes were uprated Girling discs and the wheels were lightweight Borranis. Best of all, the 3.7-litre straight-six was fitted with a new cylinder head featuring twin spark plugs per cylinder, which helped lift peak power from 240 to 302bhp.

The results were dramatic. The 0–60mph time tumbled from around 8 seconds to a whisker over 6, while the top speed rose from 140 to a genuine 150mph. At Silverstone, in the hands of Stirling Moss, the prototype won its very first race, presaging a long career in front-line motorsport.

Needless to say, as a road car nothing much could touch it – it was a whole two years before Jaguar would launch the E-type. Even today, the GT's performance is exhilarating, and on a twisting road you can sense how much more eager it is to turn into a corner, how much more nimble than a regular DB4 or 5. Yes, the steering and brakes in particular still demand exertion, and the four-speed DB gearbox can be a bit 'notchy', but the more you put in, the more you get out, and the rewards in a GT are immense. Sharp, keen and intense, it's a DB4 with more urgency and athleticism. In fact there's only one thing better than looking at a DB4 GT. And that's driving one.

SPECIFICATIONS

Years produced: 1960–63 **Engine:** In-line straight-six, 3,670cc **Max power:** 314bhp @ 6,000rpm
Max torque: 278lb ft @ 5,400rpm **0–60mph:** 6.1sec **Max speed:** 154mph
Price: £5,470/$15,316 new, £10 million+/$12.4 million+ today

1960

DB4 GT ZAGATO

Often cited as one of the most beautiful cars of all time, the rare, ultra-lightweight Zagato-bodied GT is as exotic as Astons get

S o much has been written about Zagato's take on the DB4 GT, it's almost impossible to steer clear of cliché. History, rarity and value have only served to augment its significance and desirability, while its beauty remains impervious to the passage of time. Few cars have such tautness and purity of form, fewer still such perfect proportions. It's a truly captivating sight.

With gossamer-thin aluminium bodies hand-formed by Zagato's artisan panel beaters, it's inevitable that no two DB4 GTZs are identical, but the car you see here is more distinctive than most, with a more pronounced beak, softly contoured grille and a striking chrome bead that begins where there would normally be an Aston Martin 'strake' and runs the length of the doors. DB4GT/0200/R was the first built and the car that featured at the 1960 Earls Court motor show. It also enjoyed a distinguished racing career.

Approaching this iconic car with the intent to drive it feels thrilling, slightly surreal and rather intimidating. The first thing that strikes you is its daintiness. It really is small, and when you pull on the driver's door, it feels laughably light, swinging on its hinges as though filled with helium. The seat is tiny but beautifully sculpted, with a low, curving back and a pair of buttresses that provide a little lateral support but generally leave you feeling rather exposed. The big, three-spoke steering wheel feels fabulous in your hands.

A couple of pumps on the throttle, a twist of the unpretentious ignition key hanging from the centre of the black, crackle-finish dashboard and the straight-six kicks into life, its meaty pulse fidgeting the stationary DB4 on its springs and filling the cockpit with a heady miasma of burnt and unburnt hydrocarbons. Bliss.

49

With a little trepidation you snick the thin gearstick across the tight, well-defined H-pattern gate into first, release the fly-off handbrake, tickle the throttle and ease in the clutch before moving away without any fuss or racy hissy fits. At low speed the sensations you get are alien to those of a modern car. The unassisted steering feels a bit dead and disconnected around the straight-ahead. Over bumps that a 21st-century car would simply absorb, the DB4 shimmies as the energy of the wheels hitting potholes is transmitted into the structure of the car. With experience you come to appreciate that this is what makes old cars feel alive and new cars feel numb, but if you're only used to modern machines and their miraculous structural rigidity, cosseting refinement qualities and flattering, power-assisted controls, you're almost certainly in for a culture shock.

Fittingly, the great joy of driving the DB4 Zagato comes with speed. The jittery ride settles and the disconnected steering tingles with life and feel. You don't steer it so much as nudge it through corners, your initial input setting you on a graceful course from apex to exit. It feels light and lithe, dancing on its tyre-treads like a speedboat coming up onto the plane. You can place it just so, exploiting the improved balance, agility and precision it enjoys over a regular DB4. That gloriously gutsy straight-six snorts and howls as only a motor fed by thirsty carburettors can. Always pulling strongly, but with a perceptible uplift in enthusiasm when fuelling and engine revs hit their sweet spot, it really gets up and goes.

And that's the miracle of this car: when hustled as intended, it drives even better than it looks.

SPECIFICATIONS

Years produced: 1962 **Engine:** In-line straight-six, 3,996cc **Max power:** 327bhp @ 6,000rpm
Max torque: 290lb ft @ 5,300rpm **0–60mph:** n/a
Max speed: c.180mph **Price:** £10 million+/ $12.4 million+ today

DP212

Aston Martin returned to Le Mans in the early 1960s with the DP212,

the first of a short series of fast but flawed 'Project Cars'

With Le Mans won, Aston Martin officially retired from racing at the end of 1959, though it was happy to supply lightweight versions of the DB4 to privateers. Aston dealers, though, wanted to see a proper works effort at Le Mans to boost sales. And so Design Project 212 was born – part engineering test-bed, part works racer, loosely based on the DB4 GT with its twin-plug version of the 3.7-litre Tadek Marek straight-six.

For 1962, Le Mans was allowing a 4-litre GT prototype category, so the engine was taken out to 4 litres and given a trio of 50DCO Webers, in which form it made 327bhp. The chassis was further lightened, there was a de Dion tube in place of the GT's live axle, and it was all clothed in aerodynamic bodywork, initially with a long, tapering tail, designed to give it extra speed on the Mulsanne.

The extra power and smoother shape paid dividends: the DP212 was certainly rapid, if not particularly stable above 160mph. With Graham Hill at the wheel, it led the first lap and was lying second to the winning prototype Ferrari 330P at the end of the first hour, but a fractured oil line ended its race. Back in the UK, it went to Silverstone for high-speed testing and it was discovered that a flat 'Kamm' tail and spoiler would aid stability and increase top speed – a similar tail treatment was later carried over to the DB6.

The DP212 returned to Le Mans in 1963 but only ran in practice, where it was reported to have hit 187mph. And that was the end of its period racing story, though it has recently enjoyed success in historic racing, including a brilliant win in the 2013 Goodwood TT revival. Simon Hadfield, who drove it that day, described it like this: 'It has a nice balance. Through Madgwick, as it takes a set and it's just a little bit sideways, you're hard on the power and you can take that balance all the way through to the second apex. That is gorgeous, the most

sensational feeling. Unless a car talks to you, you can't commit, you can't go out to where the air gets thin.'

How does DP212 compare with a regular DB4 GT? 'It's just better. It's a bit lighter. The little flip on the tail that they added in '63, that helps. The car's just a little bit more stable. With the DB4 GT, it feels more like a converted road car. This is a racing car. A little bit quicker in a straight line, a little bit better everywhere. In their day these really were the cutting edge.'

The pace that the DP212 showed on debut at Le Mans in 1962 was enough to convince Aston Martin to build further Project Cars for the 1963 race: two DP214s and a single DP215.

The DP214s were substantially modified in the interests of lightness: the GT engine was bored out slightly to 3,750cc and moved further back in the chassis to aid agility, while the body incorporated lessons learned with the 212. In the race, both 214s retired with piston failure. One returned in 1964 but was disqualified in the 18th hour for taking on oil too early while lying ninth. The sister car was scrapped after a crash at the Nürburgring in 1964 in which the driver, Brian Hetreed, was fatally injured.

The DP215 was to be entered in the prototype class and was originally intended to carry a new V8 engine. In its place was a 4-litre dry-sump version of the twin-plug straight-six, mated to the transaxle from the DBR1. That was to be its undoing, the transaxle failing in the third hour after a spell in the lead.

Both the 214 and 215 were officially recorded as exceeding 300kph (186mph) on the Mulsanne – the first cars to do so – while, in practice in the 215, Phil Hill was clocked at 198.6mph. This extraordinary figure guaranteed a place in Aston Martin folklore for the Project Cars – among the most enigmatic and intriguing of all Astons.

The three surviving Project Cars: from left to right, DP215, DP212 and DP214.

DB5

The DB5 isn't just The Bond Car, it's also a fabulous machine in its own right

SPECIFICATIONS

Years produced: 1963–66 **Engine:** In-line straight-six, 3,995cc **Max power:** 282bhp @ 5,500rpm
Max torque: 288lb ft @ 3,850rpm **0–60mph:** 8.0sec **Max speed:** 145mph
Price: £4,248/$12,775, £600,000+/$746,800 (convertible at least double) today

I n reality it was just another evolution of the DB4, which had been slowly evolving ever since its 1958 introduction, but Aston Martin decided there was enough that was new about its latest model to give it a brand-new name, and so in 1963 it launched the DB5. It duly received the usual plaudits from the press, but no particular fanfare. At the time it was, indeed, just the latest car from Newport Pagnell. It was only after Aston Martin lent a prototype to EON Productions for its latest Bond film, *Goldfinger*, that the DB5 began to gain a significance that would eventually overshadow all other cars to wear the famous wings.

So, what was different about the DB5? Most significantly, an enlarged, 4-litre version of the now-familiar all-alloy straight-six engine (up from 3.7 litres), giving a quoted – and almost certainly optimistic – 282bhp on triple SU carbs, or, for the Vantage engine, 314bhp on triple Webers. It was joined soon after production started by a five-speed ZF gearbox in place of the old four-speed DB unit. Other changes included an alternator, tinted glass, dual-circuit Girling disc brakes with twin servos, and a new instrument layout, while luxury touches like electric windows and air conditioning joined the options list for the first time, reflecting a change of emphasis from the early, more overtly sporting DB4s. Visually, there were the fared-in headlamps, though the DB4 GT and some end-of-line DB4s also had these.

On the road today, the extra torque of the 4-litre engine makes progress effortless compared with a standard DB4, while the five-speed gearbox does similarly good things for the car's GT credentials, though it's not a particularly sweet-shifting gearbox, and downright obstinate when cold.

Handling-wise, individual cars vary hugely, depending on tyres, whether they've had a power steering conversion and/or a handling kit, and so on. What's generally true is that the DB5 is too heavy to be a genuine out-and-out sports car, responding best if you ease it into the turn and then accelerate through, tweaking the steering as the tyres move around. It's a class act and a friendly one – mostly. Drive it hard on the right tyres and it'll four-wheel-drift through a turn and, being long and relatively narrow, the rear will slide wide, but it's predictable and recoverable, although heavy (especially with the original non-assisted steering).

As with the DB4, there was an extremely pretty – and rare – Convertible version. To compensate for the loss of rigidity, strengthening was added beneath the rear seat pan and the recess for the folded hood, and in the sills. There were other, subtle differences: the Convertible had a more upright windscreen, making it 2.5cm (1in) taller than that of the saloon.

Needless to say, today these are among the most desirable of all Aston Martins, and this desirability inevitably makes them among the most expensive to buy. At an auction in 2015, Bonhams established a new world record price for a Convertible of £1,430,715/$2,217,608. Considering that price was for a standard-tune car; a Vantage-engined example would today, no doubt, fetch more. Even the far more common coupés now regularly go for over half a million pounds/$622,500 – and always in excess of that, of course, if painted Silver Birch…

DB5

1966
DB6

With its controversial 'Kamm' tail and softer GT character, the DB6 is slightly overshadowed by

the 4 and 5, but it's still a great car

SPECIFICATIONS:

Years produced: 1966–70 **Engine:** In-line straight-six, 3,995cc **Max power:** 325bhp @ 5,750rpm (Vantage)
Max torque: 290lb ft @ 4,500rpm **0–60mph:** c.7.0sec **Max speed:** c.150mph
Price: £4,998/$15,00 new in 1966, £350,000+/$435,650+ (Volante at least double) today

The **DB5** was the toughest of acts to follow, but nothing was better for blasting down to the south of France in the late 1960s than a DB6. It combined all the strengths of the DB4 and DB5 with increased interior space, extra luggage capacity and greater high-speed stability. So why is it still undervalued? Comparative ubiquity is one reason. By the time production ended in November 1970, close to 2,000 had been built. Not a huge quantity, but almost twice the number of DB5s that left Newport Pagnell.

While the DB5 had been a simple evolution of the DB4, the DB6 was a genuinely new model. By adding almost 10cm (4in) to the wheelbase and raising the roofline over the rear seats, it was now a passable four-seater. Visually, the front bumper was now split, with a slatted grille for the oil cooler below it. At the rear, David Brown and his team agonized over the 'Kamm' tail (carried over from the Project racers), fretting that it would alienate some customers. But they couldn't ignore wind tunnel tests, which showed it reduced lift at the rear wheels by over 30 per cent.

Under the skin, the mechanical package was pretty much carried over from the DB5. The Vantage version, with triple Webers and slightly racier cams, gave 325bhp, while the regular engine made 282bhp on SUs. In late 1969 the MKII version arrived with lightly flared wheel-arch lips to accommodate wider wheels, and the option of electronic fuel injection, a first on a British car. There was also a super-rare (and now super-valuable) convertible, called the Volante.

Driving a thoroughly fettled DB6 today reminds you just how distant and disconnected modern cars can be. In fact this is a surprisingly delicate car to guide, the thin-rimmed steering wheel wriggling gently in your hands as the front wheels read the road as if it were Braille. The gearbox is a joy, its shift precise and confidence-inspiring. The ratios give the DB6 fabulous reach, yet offer enough get-up-and-go to punch you down the road with surprising vigour.

Handling-wise, the DB6 has great fluidity. Modern sports cars have tremendous levels of grip and iron-fisted damping that encourage an aggressive, binary style of driving. This car has ample roadholding, but it allows itself to flow more freely. Once you've gained confidence in its ability to stop, steer and stick to the tarmac, you relax your grip of the steering wheel a little and let the DB6 do its thing. Sheer joy.

1966
Lola-Aston

By the mid-1960s, Aston Martin was planning to replace its straight-six with a new V8 engine.
This Le Mans racer would be a test-bed

T he **Lola-Aston** project grew out of John Surtees' dream of winning Le Mans with an all-British car. By 1966, the seven-time motorcycle and recent F1 Grand Prix champion had established his own racing team, which had enjoyed considerable success in CanAm racing with the Lola T70. Now he had his sights set on the World Sportscar Championship and Le Mans. But the British-built Lola was powered by American V8s, and Surtees wanted a British engine, too. So when he heard Aston Martin was developing a V8 of its own, talks began and a deal was done.

The new all-aluminium Aston V8 already looked more aristocratic than the iron Chevrolet engine and had a pair of double overhead camshafts instead of pushrods, just like a Ferrari. Like a proper race engine, in other words.

Tadek Marek had begun design work on the V8 back in 1963 but the first engine didn't run until July 1965, breathing through four downdraught IDA Weber carburettors to develop 275bhp from 4,806cc. Surtees' experience with Ferrari had already convinced him that there was no substitute for capacity, and Aston's development team was persuaded to increase the engine's bore to give a total of 4,983cc, which also made room for bigger inlet valves. With the Lola-Surtees-

Aston partnership confirmed, Aston set about development and built a batch of ten special race engines featuring magnesium cylinder blocks, instead of aluminium, in a bid to save more weight. By the autumn of 1966, power output had risen to a claimed 420bhp at 6,500rpm.

The team went to Le Mans in June 1967 with two cars: chassis SL73/101 for English 'coming man' Chris Irwin and the South African Piet de Klerk, and SL73/121 for Surtees and David Hobbs. The 121 boasted fuel injection and a longer aluminium tail in an attempt to improve on the 186mph maximum speed recorded at the Le Mans test day earlier in the year, when the Fords were doing well over 200mph.

History records that Surtees qualified 13th but went out of the race after three laps with a holed piston, while the sister car suffered engine dramas from the off, eventually retiring after two and a half hours when these became terminal. Surtees and Aston blamed each other for the failures, and the project ended acrimoniously after just a year. It was, however, a useful part of the new engine's development: there was no doubt that when the road version eventually appeared, it was better as a result of the race experience. As for the Lola-Aston, it was a tantalizing case of what might have been…

SPECIFICATIONS

Years produced: 1966–67 **Engine:** V8, 4,983cc **Max power:** 420bhp @ 6,500rpm
Max torque: n/a **0–60mph:** n/a
Max speed: c.190mph **Price:** n/a

Lola-Aston

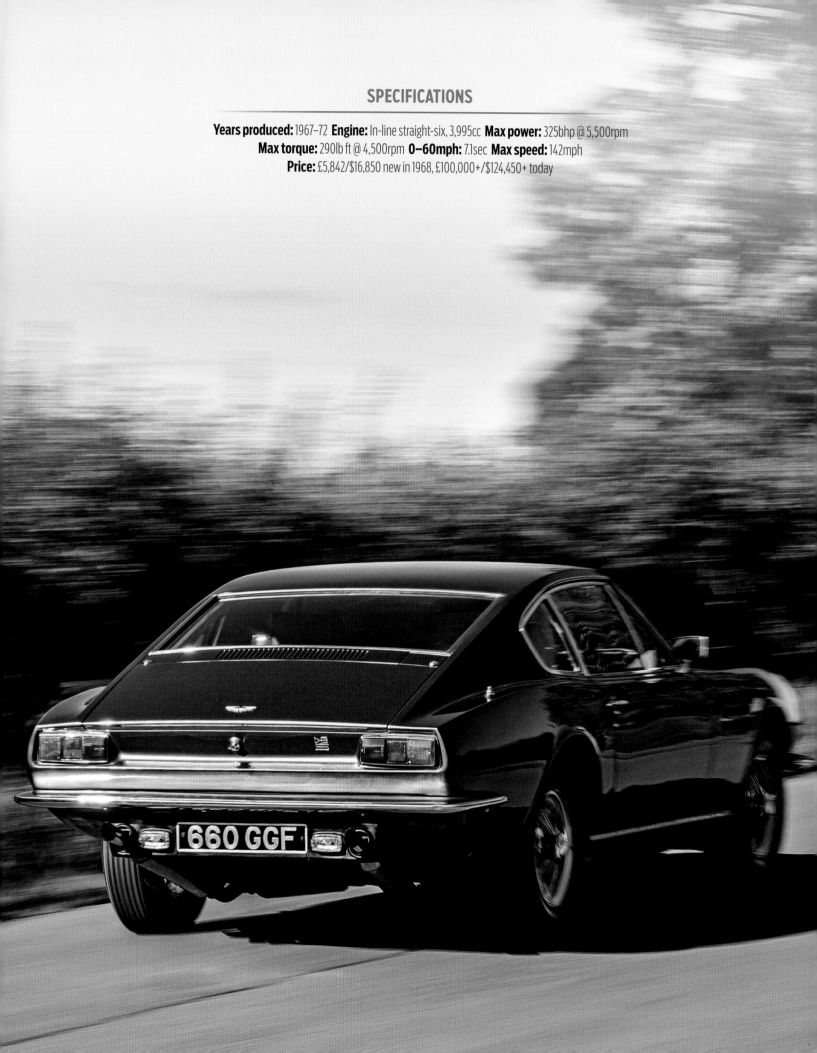

SPECIFICATIONS

Years produced: 1967–72 **Engine:** In-line straight-six, 3,995cc **Max power:** 325bhp @ 5,500rpm
Max torque: 290lb ft @ 4,500rpm **0–60mph:** 7.1sec **Max speed:** 142mph
Price: £5,842/$16,850 new in 1968, £100,000+/$124,450+ today

1967

DBS

The new V8 engine wasn't ready, so the DBS had to launch with the familiar straight-six from the DB6

When the DB6 was announced in 1965, its planned replacement was already in the early stages of development. Styling partner Touring of Milan came up with a concept, but it was deeply uninspiring, so the gig went to in-house stylist William Towns, who had recently joined Aston Martin from Rover. Towns created a masterpiece, even if Aston patron David Brown demanded it gain a bonnet bulge after Towns had been specifically instructed not to include one!

A prototype was up and running by July 1967, powered by the firm's enduring straight-six because Tadek Marek's V8 was not yet production-ready. Without sufficient time to create a new platform from scratch, the basic DB6 frame was adapted for the new car: widened by 11.4cm (4½in) and with the wheelbase lengthened by 2.5cm (1in) to allow the engine to sit low down behind the front crossmember. Wishbone suspension at the front was carried over from the outgoing car, but at the rear a de Dion tube was introduced for the first time on an Aston in place of the old live axle.

Despite the absence of the much anticipated V8, the DBS ('S' reportedly standing for Sport) was warmly received by the press. Although its greater weight meant it was a smidge slower than the DB6 (which actually continued to be built alongside the new model for a year or so), it was still a 140mph car and its ride and handling were a significant improvement.

Today, the DBS feels like a big car, even though by modern standards it's positively dainty. It sounds sublime under load, too. The 3,995cc straight-six emits a lovely, aggressive bark that can only be blue-blooded. The ZF five-speed gearbox doesn't like to be rushed, but the ratios are near-perfect. It's a lovely cruiser, too, trickling along with barely a murmur.

The Aston's heft is all too obvious in tight corners, but the Adwest power steering is light, with decent feedback through the wheel. The ride is firm without being harsh, and history informs you that, once the tail starts moving, it will probably take out a small cottage before righting itself.

But you don't approach the DBS looking for a back-road tearaway. It's an urbane GT in the truest sense and, as such, utterly captivating.

1969
DBS V8

In 1969 the DBS finally got the V8 engine it had been designed around and
Aston had a new world-beater on its hands

The six-cylinder DBS had been well received, but what everyone really wanted to experience was the same car with Aston Martin's magnificent new 5.3-litre quad-cam V8 engine. When the press finally got their hands on the first DBS V8s in the autumn of 1969, they were not disappointed.

This was power and performance on a new level for Aston Martin. Indeed, the DBS's original wire-spoke wheels couldn't handle the torque, so Aston had to replace them with chunky alloys. These early fuel-injected DBS V8s recorded 0–60mph times of less than 6 seconds and a top speed of over 160mph. As *Autocar* reported in July 1971: 'There can be no doubt that the Aston Martin DBS V8 is one of the fastest cars we have ever tested.'

Even today, the DBS V8 looks, feels and sounds magnificent. Inside there are big, comfy seats and plenty of room to work. Ahead, framed by the simple, three-spoked steering wheel, there's a splendid array of Smiths dials, surely one of every dial that Mr Smith could supply in the late 1960s and early 1970s. Looking out, there's brilliant vision in all directions, particularly the view over the bonnet, from the

subtle bulge rising in the centre to the razor edges of the wings.

When the V8 catches, it sounds busy, sophisticated, so different from the lumpy hollering of its American pushrod equivalents. Engage dogleg first, release the fly-off handbrake down by your left shin and ease away. The pedals feel fearsomely heavy at first, but once you're on the move you don't seem to notice – though it might be different in traffic.

The steering is exactly as a servo system should be, offering useful but discreet assistance. The ZF gearbox has a long throw but a well-oiled, satisfying feel. The stiff throttle takes some getting used to, but as confidence grows it becomes second nature to blip it on down changes. The brakes – vented Girling discs – have a rather dead feeling initially. In fact the stopping power's decent enough, but you're always conscious of the weight of the car.

The chassis is never sports-car flickable, but fundamentally well sorted and nicely in tune front-to-rear. Get it turned-in and settled and you can pour in the power in satisfying fashion. It rides well, too. Really big bumps do catch the rear out, but it's a whole lot more composed than a DB4, 5 or 6. This truly was a new-age Aston.

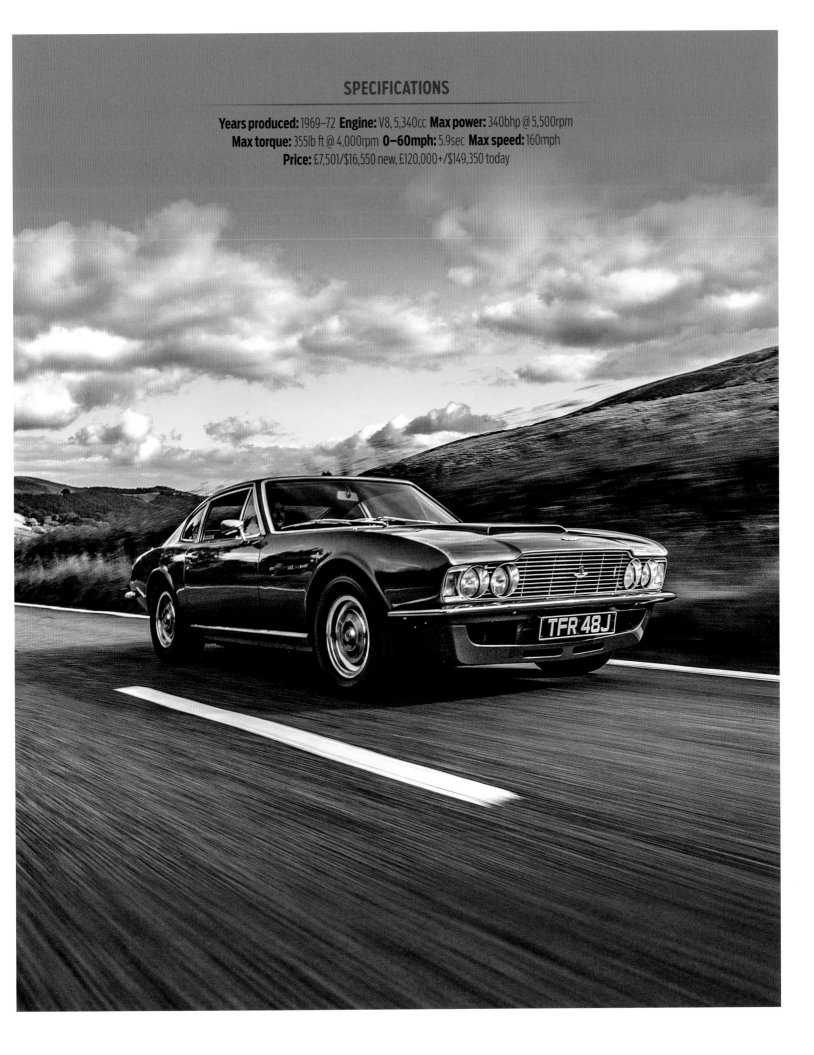

SPECIFICATIONS

Years produced: 1969–72 **Engine:** V8, 5,340cc **Max power:** 340bhp @ 5,500rpm
Max torque: 355lb ft @ 4,000rpm **0–60mph:** 5.9sec **Max speed:** 160mph
Price: £7,501/$16,550 new, £120,000+/$149,350 today

1969
Lagonda V8 Series 1

Designed to sit alongside the DBS V8 was a four-door version, badged as a Lagonda

SPECIFICATIONS

Years produced: 1969 (prototype) and 1972–76 **Engine:** V8, 5,340cc **Max power:** c.300bhp @ 5,000rpm
Max torque: c.350lb ft @ 4,000rpm **0–60mph:** c.7.0sec **Max speed:** c.140mph
Price: c.£15,000/$36,000 new, £400,000+/$497,900+ today

Back in the early 1960s, David Brown had revived the Lagonda badge on the Rapide, a DB4-based four-door saloon. Blighted by a curious frontal treatment with sloped quad headlamps and outlandish grilles, it struggled to sell: just 54 were built between 1961 and 1964. Undaunted, in the late 1960s the recently knighted Sir David commissioned another four-door Lagonda, this time based around the DBS V8. It wasn't exactly a runaway success…

The car you see here is the prototype, which Sir David used as his own personal transport for several years. After he relinquished control of the company, the idea was revived by the new owners of Aston Martin, who, in 1974, officially launched the Lagonda V8 saloon, with a new grille reminiscent of the Rapide (possibly not the best move) and a stiff asking price of £15,000/$36,000. Alas, it was no more successful than the Rapide had been – in two years of production just seven were sold.

The car here, chassis number MP230/1, was registered on 5 May 1969 but only revealed to the press on 16 January 1970, after the regular DBS V8 had made its public debut. It seemed a perfectly comfortable extension of the DBS brand, as well it should, given that William Towns had conceived the two styles of body at the same time.

Open a rear door and you'll discover headroom that's less than generous, but there's enough legroom to lounge quite luxuriously, even though half of the wheelbase increase has gone on a bigger boot.

To drive, the Lagonda simply feels like the longer, heavier, less wieldy Aston V8 that it is. It's still quick, while the rapid descent of the fuel gauge's reading seems as normal as the woofle of the V8. The small steering wheel and hefty assistance help disguise the mass in the bends, and you can soon corner with a verve likely to ruin your rear passenger's assimilation of the financial pages. Through all this, it rides in a civilized enough fashion, but its genes will never allow it to be truly cosseting.

In 1976 the Lagonda V8 saloon was quietly dropped from the price lists. Another, far more outlandish – but, ultimately, far more successful – Lagonda was by then a twinkle in the management's eye…

ASTONS IN BOND

From DB5 to DB10, James Bond and Aston Martin have been inextricably linked. But one of cinema's greatest double acts nearly didn't happen at all...

The time has long since passed when you could separate James Bond and Aston Martin. Sure, other brands have bought their sprinkle of Ian Fleming fairy-dust, with large cheques exchanged for supplying 007's company wheels, but nothing feels or looks so right as the world's most famous secret agent behind the wheel of an Aston. Conclusive proof of the phenomenon came during early screenings of *Skyfall*, when audiences erupted into cheers as the DB5 made its first appearance. Cars shouldn't have that effect on cinema-goers, but Bond's car, or more specifically, Bond's Aston, is different.

Hard to believe now, but Aston Martin was initially reluctant to supply a car when EON Productions started filming its third and most ambitious Bond picture yet, 1964's *Goldfinger*. Fortunately, the management at Newport Pagnell eventually relented and, in January 1964, released the surplus DB5 prototype, chassis number DP216/1, at that stage still painted in original Dubonnet Rosso. Registered BMT 216A, it was kitted out by John Stears of EON with Ken Adam's gadgets and re-emerged with the now famous Silver Birch paint job. Known as the Effects Car, it was used for all the close-up shots.

But it wasn't the only DB5 used in the filming of *Goldfinger*. Soon after, Aston also loaned EON a standard production-spec DB5 for the regular driving scenes and all the high-speed work. This car, DB5/1486/R (registration FMP 7B), has to this day been known as the Road Car. And it was the Road Car that returned in the follow-up film, *Thunderball*, by now fitted with the full set of gadgets itself.

When, in 1997, the Effects Car was stolen from a secure storage unit in Florida, the Road Car became the most authentic, significant and valuable Bond DB5 in existence. In 2010, it was sold at auction to an American collector for £2.6 million/$4.1 million – its value today doubtless rather more.

Licence to thrill: DB10 and the definitive Bond Aston, DB5

But it's by no means the only Bond DB5 out there. As 007 fever gripped the world in the mid-1960s, EON purchased two further DB5s and had them fully kitted out with the famous gadgets for press and publicity duties. And in the 1990s, when it was decided to resurrect the DB5 for Pierce Brosnan's Bond in *Goldeneye*, no fewer than three fresh cars were conscripted. One of these, chassis number DB5/1481/R, is owned by EON to this day, and would go on to star in *Tomorrow Never Dies*, *Skyfall* and *Spectre*.

For most Bond fans – especially those of us who spent formative childhood years playing with the Corgi toy version of the DB5, marvelling at what it must be like to have a car fitted with machine guns and an ejector seat – the definitive Bond Aston will always be the DB5. But, of course, it's not the only Bond Aston.

For the production of 1969's *On Her Majesty's Secret Service*, Aston Martin was asked to loan two examples of its latest model – the William Towns-styled DBS, to be driven by the new Australian Bond, George Lazenby. Unlike the tricked-up DB5, the DBSs were pretty much factory-standard, with the exception of a glove-box-mounted rifle.

Though the latest Aston's appearances in *OHMSS* were fleeting, those scenes bookend the narrative: one that begins with a suicide attempt and ends with the most downbeat finale in the Bond cannon when 007's new bride dies in a hail of bullets while seated in the Aston.

The car used for most of the driving shots was press demonstrator DBS/5234/R, registered GKX 8G, initially fitted with a standard engine but uprated to Vantage spec midway through 1969. Once free of filming and press duties, it was sold to the British School of Motoring for its performance driving course!

A DBS would also appear, albeit fleetingly, in 1971's *Diamonds Are Forever*. It can be glimpsed in the background of Q's workshop, apparently being fitted with a set of missiles. Alas, that's its only appearance.

It was more than 15 years before EON renewed Bond's association with Aston Martin for 1987's *The Living Daylights*. At the start of the film, we see our hero, played for the first time by Timothy Dalton, driving a V8 Volante with Cumberland Grey coachwork. In real life, this car was, in fact, the personal transport of Victor Gauntlett, chairman of Aston Martin Lagonda at the time.

In the film, the Volante reappears in Q's workshop, where the viewer is asked to believe that it is being 'winterized' with the addition of a hardtop. In fact it was switched to a regular AM V8 saloon, which appears in the rest of the film, now fully loaded with Q goodies, including, most famously, a rocket propulsion system and a set of skis for driving on a frozen lake. The producers of the film obtained three well-used examples for stunt work, and several glass-fibre replicas were also built.

For the 20th film in the series, 2002's *Die Another Day*, Pierce Brosnan's 007 was given the very latest V12 Vanquish, finished in Tungsten Silver with Charcoal leather to echo the colour combo of the *Goldfinger* DB5.

The Ford Motor Company, owner of AML at the time, came to a special agreement with EON Productions and MGM whereby the giant car maker provided

Cinema audiences cheered when the DB5 reappeared in 2012's *Skyfall* a significant quantity of assorted cars, including seven V12 Vanquishes. Four pre-production cars were extensively rebuilt to provide the special effects, while three rather more standard production cars would be used for close-ups and interiors, the so-called 'hero' cars.

The four special effects cars needed to be fitted with a four-wheel-drive system for the action sequences shot on a frozen lake in Iceland, so the Vanquish bodyshells were fitted with 300bhp Ford Boss 302 V8s mounted as far back in the chassis as possible. This allowed sufficient room for the fitting of a front differential and drive shafts from the Ford Explorer, plus space for weaponry behind the grille. These 120mph Aston/Ford hybrids were fitted with roll-cages, and, since the frozen lake was only just thick enough to drive on following a 'warm' winter, concealed flotation devices were also added in case the ice gave way under the cars. Another interesting feature of the four-wheel-drive Vanquish was the automatic gearbox that allowed for 120mph in both forward and reverse.

In 2006, the debut of another new Bond – Daniel Craig – in *Casino Royale* coincided with the first appearance of another new Bond Aston, the DB9-based DBS. In fact, at the time the DBS was chosen as 007's new pool car, it existed only as a styling buck. Yet within a little over three months, Aston's prototype workshop had managed to turn out and deliver two working hero cars to be used in close-ups and for regular driving sequences. Based on DB9 development cars, they had a unique 2+0 configuration with space behind the seats for a race helmet, a fire extinguisher and a gun holder – all features never intended for production cars. AML also supplied three former development DB9s for use as DBS lookalike stunt cars.

On screen, the DBS famously meets its demise in a spectacular barrel roll on the country roads of Montenegro (in reality, the Hill Route at the Millbrook test facility in Bedfordshire). The first stunt car refused to co-operate, so the second was installed with a nitrogen-powered ram to punch the tarmac at the correct moment to start the car rolling. It worked so well that the results were even more spectacular than the stunt team had imagined. When stunt driver Adam Kirley stepped from the wreckage, mercifully unhurt, he'd established a new Guinness World Record for most cannon rolls in a car, achieving an astonishing seven complete turns.

Bond was reunited with the DBS for 2008's *Quantum of Solace*. Ten brand-new production DBSs were supplied, the first four for special effects, the remainder as hero cars for close-ups, interior shots and promotional work. It was the first time actual production cars had been supplied for special effects knowing fully that they would be trashed during filming. Two of these were lost during the production, one when it plunged into Lake Garda in a freak accident that the driver was fortunate to survive.

These contemporary Astons were an excellent fit for a new, grittier era of Bond movies, but fans still cheered when Daniel Craig pulled open the doors of his garage to reveal his beloved DB5 in 2012's *Skyfall*. As well as two right-hand-drive DB5s, a Porsche 928-based replica and a sophisticated fifth-scale model were also needed for filming. One of the cars was DB5/1484/R, purchased by EON in 1995 and appearing in its third Bond film. The other was DB5/2007/R, which was awaiting restoration at

Aston boss Victor Gauntlett lent his own V8 Volante for 1987's *The Living Daylights*

Aston Martin Works when it was chosen for stardom. The beige interior was quickly recoloured black and the coachwork repainted from Goodwood Green to Silver Birch. The owner, a Works customer and noted Aston collector, was no doubt thrilled to find he was now the owner of a genuine Bond car!

For 2015's *Spectre*, Bond could have quite easily found himself in a current Vanquish. That's certainly what most Bond – and Aston – fans were expecting, but then news broke that the next Bond Aston would be something all new. Something called the DB10.

To say the DB10 was created specially for Bond from scratch would be stretching the truth a little – underneath the carbon-fibre skin was basically a stretched and widened V8 Vantage – but the fact remains that this spectacular new car took Aston's relationship with Bond to a whole new level.

Starting life as a concept in the Aston design studio, the clay model was spotted by director Sam Mendes on a visit to Gaydon. 'That's the car I want in the movie!' he declared, giving the engineers just a little over a year to turn the model into a living car.

So the DB10 was hand-built in a strictly limited batch of just ten cars exclusively for EON and never intended for sale. Most were used for stunt work, but four were hero cars that could be used for the close-ups. One example was later auctioned for charity and bought by a private individual for £2.4 million/$3 million, though the DB10 wasn't actually homologated for road use. Best of all, and in a perfect case of life imitating art, the ten cars were built by a department called Q Advanced Engineering. The Bond/Aston connection had never been stronger.

Above: DB10 was specially created for Bond

Right: one of four 'hero cars' used for close-ups

THE V8
YEARS

The V8 Years –
Introduction

The post-David Brown era was a turbulent time for Aston Martin and yet it still produced some truly great cars

T he early 1970s weren't the best years for Aston Martin. The DB era had ended when Sir David sold up in 1972, and new owners Company Holdings were, by their own admission, 'not car people'. As if to confirm their lack of empathy, when the DBS V8 was relaunched under the new regime, it was to be known simply as the AM V8, the 'DB' part having been dropped, they said, 'for marketing reasons'. And when they relaunched the lower-powered six-cylinder model, they called it the Vantage, the name formerly reserved for the high-performance versions. The omens weren't good.

To be fair, boss William Willson and his team kept the factory open at a time when political and economic forces were conspiring against makers of expensive high-performance

motorcars. But, at the end of 1974, they were finally forced to throw in the towel, the company went into receivership and the factory closed. There was a real risk it wouldn't reopen.

It took a consortium, led by American Peter Sprague, to rescue Aston Martin in 1975 and revive the marque's fortunes. However, production wouldn't restart until early 1976, and then only in tiny numbers as the factory struggled to convince suppliers that it wasn't about to fold again.

Short-term salvation came in the most unlikely form. Chief stylist William Towns had sketched a proposal for a new Lagonda: an impossibly low, lean and angular saloon, the likes of which had never been seen before. Sprague and his partners – Canadian George Minden and Englishman Alan Curtis – loved it. And when, in October 1976, the new Lagonda

'Bert' Bertelli and new boss William Willson in 1974

Aston's darkest hour: production suspended in 1974

Chief stylist William Towns at his drawing board

Towns' wedge-shaped Lagonda caused a sensation in 1976

made its debut at the Earls Court motor show, deposits poured in. Aston Martin was back.

In the late 1970s, the rejuvenated marque was able to update the Aston V8, launch Volante and Vantage versions and even build an extraordinary 200mph supercar called Bulldog.

But, as ever, financial strife wasn't far away, and in 1981 an oil crisis hit sales and threatened the company's survival once again. The saviour this time was a larger-than-life British businessman, Victor Gauntlett, who led a new consortium to keep Aston Martin afloat. Over the next decade, with a series of backers, including the Livanos family of Greek shipping magnates, Gauntlett reinvigorated the old marque. There was a return to Le Mans, a new collaboration with Italian styling house Zagato to produce the fearsome V8 Zagato and, in

1988, a brand-new Aston, the Virage, to replace the 20-year-old V8 range.

By then, Ford had taken a 75 per cent stake in Aston Martin and was looking at ways to make the company (whisper it) profitable. The result would be the DB7, announced in 1993 with Sir David Brown's blessing. This truly was the car that transformed Aston Martin's fortunes, selling in greater numbers than anyone associated with the pre-Ford company had ever dared dream.

At the end of the 1990s, Aston unveiled a concept for a new flagship car, to be called the Vanquish, which would use an innovative new aluminium chassis. As the last of the old V8-engine cars left the factory in 2000, a new era for Aston Martin was dawning.

Victor Gauntlett (left) with John Martin, son of company founder Lionel

Newport Pagnell Astons were always hand-finished

SPECIFICATIONS

Years produced: 1972–90 **Engine:** V8, 5,340cc **Max power:** c.300bhp @ 6,000rpm
Max torque: c.320lb ft @ 3,000rpm **0–60mph:** c.6.0sec **Max speed:** c.155mph
Price: £9,592/$22,000 new in 1973, £100,000+/$124,400+ today

1972
AM V8

With new owners at the helm, the DBS V8 morphed into the AM V8. After a sticky start,

it evolved into a fine GT and a true modern classic

Times were turbulent at Newport Pagnell in the early 1970s and, as a result, the build quality of the cars was – how shall we put this? – patchy. When *Motor* tried an AM V8, its testers reported that the bolts retaining the final drive unit became detached, the transistorized ignition amplifier failed, as did the air-conditioning thermostat, swarf was found in a carburettor, and the clutch required attention.

And yet the road testers raved about it! Because, despite everything, the AM V8 was the fastest, most accomplished high-performance luxury GT of its day – and in its various guises would remain in production for almost two decades.

As the DBS V8 evolved into the AM V8, it was decided to ditch the tricky-to-service Bosch fuel injection for a quartet of twin-choke Weber carburettors (necessitating a bigger bonnet scoop). It certainly didn't harm the performance: in fact *Motor*'s 0–60mph time of 5.7 seconds was almost half a second quicker than they'd achieved with the injected car. Even if top speed was 5mph down at 155mph, it was still one of the world's quickest GT cars.

In 1978 came the 'Oscar India' (aviation code for OI or October Introduction) model: still carb-fed, so retaining a big bonnet-scoop, but with a host of detail improvements, subtle body changes, including a neat tail-spoiler, and, inside, a more sumptuous feel, with lashings of glossy wood veneer. The final version ran from 1985 to 1989 and had Weber-Marelli electronic fuel injection (EFI), distinguished by a virtually flat bonnet.

That's an EFI in the photos, a late-1988 series-5, the final evolution of the classic V8 line. This one's on 16-inch (40.5 cm) Ronal alloys, as fitted to the contemporary Vantage, wrapped in slightly lower-profile Michelin Pilot Sports, and also benefits from a handling kit, as many now do.

So it's sharper than it would have been in period, but it's still no sports car. It gains speed steadily rather than violently, though there's still something compelling about the way it covers the ground, and something truly stirring about the induction roar when you pin the throttle.

It rides well, too. It's only when a wheel thumps into a pothole that it loses a little composure. Start to work the chassis a little harder through the turns, and it feels like the heavyweight it is. But as long as you're careful with your entry speed you can power through in a most satisfying manner. And all the time the V8 engine never stops throbbing, pulsating, burbling, dominating everything. Marvellous!

1976
Lagonda Series 2

William Towns' breathtakingly audacious Lagonda had myriad teething problems,

but somehow it rose above them all

SPECIFICATIONS

Years produced: 1979–90 **Engine:** V8, 5,340cc **Max power:** 280bhp @ 5,500rpm
Max torque: 360lb ft @ 3,000rpm **0–60mph:** 8.0sec **Max speed:** 143mph
Price: £32,620/$150,000 new in 1979, £80,000+/$110,000 today

As we know, the mid-1970s were tricky times. The AM V8 was a potent and handsome machine, but in the wake of a global oil crisis that saw a vicious spike in energy costs, thirsty GTs were hardly flying out of the door. So what do you pin your hopes on to see you through such turbulent times? Why, an outlandish, fiercely expensive, 1,815-kg (2-ton), V8-powered luxury saloon, of course.

Hindsight suggests this decision was at best optimistic, at worst suicidal; deliveries didn't commence for three years, by which time the world was in another oil crisis! Factor in single-digit fuel consumption, ambitious and hopelessly dysfunctional instrumentation and truly extraordinary William Towns styling and you have what appears to be the perfect storm of harebrained 1970s lunacy and Aston Martin's uncanny knack of powering at full throttle from the frying pan into the fire.

Yet, remarkably, history tells a different story. As deposits poured in, it's no great exaggeration to suggest that the Lagonda was the unlikely saviour of the company, and with strong sales to the Middle East, no fewer than 645 were produced between 1979 and 1990. What's more, its ability to court controversy and slacken jaws remains undiminished.

This is a luxury car in the 1970s shag-pile sense. You sit low, sunk deep into the exceptionally comfortable seat, hands resting on the small, bizarre-looking steering wheel and peering at the huge black void of a dashboard, the car's vital signs displayed via numerous red LED digital panels.

Powered by the familiar 5.3-litre V8 (fed by a quartet of Weber carburettors), the Lagonda has a quoted 280bhp and 360lb ft of torque to propel its 1,815-kg (2-ton) mass, via Chrysler's three-speed Torqueflite automatic transmission. Each prod of the accelerator shimmies the Lagonda on its soft coil springs. Pull the sliding gear selector into 'D', ease your foot from the brake to the accelerator, and the big wedge rumbles away. An involuntary smile spreads across your face. You don't so much accelerate as gain momentum, but once up to a cruising speed, it feels truly majestic. The Lagonda's appetite for corners is less ravenous, the soft suspension yielding all too soon to the surprisingly quick-witted steering, but beneath the nautical levels of roll and porcine protests from the tyres, it handles tidily, with a sweet balance of grip front to rear and an impressive agility for a car so dedicated to comfort. It's still surprising us after all these years…

1977

V8 Vantage

The original V8 Vantage – not the one that came out in 2005 – was dubbed Britain's first supercar,
and with good reason

SPECIFICATIONS

Years produced: 1977–89 **Engine:** V8, 5,340cc **Max power:** c.420bhp @ 6,000rpm
Max torque: c.400lb ft @ 5,000rpm **0–60mph:** 5.2sec **Max speed:** 170mph
Price: £20,000/$52,000 new in 1977, £250,000+/$311,000 today

T he DBS V8 of the early 1970s, and the AM V8 that it had morphed into, were fine sporting GTs, but they didn't have the fire power or the road presence to match the Italian and German supercars that were plastered over magazine covers and teenage boys' bedroom walls in the 1970s – cars like the Lamborghini Countach and Porsche Turbo. Something altogether more serious was required.

Confidence and orders slowly returned to Newport Pagnell following Aston's revival, so the engineering team under Mike Loasby began developing the high-performance V8 derivative that they'd been desperate to build. Whereas in years gone by the Vantage tag had been used to denote a tuned engine, now it would come to stand for a wholly revamped car. From the engine to the chassis to the aerodynamics, everything was pumped up and finely honed. For the first time, the Vantage was a distinct model in its own right.

Instantly recognizable by its blanked-off grille, Perspex-faired headlamps, twin additional driving lights, front air dam and boot-lid spoiler, the Vantage had road presence to spare. Meanwhile, the 5.3-litre V8 gained higher-lift camshafts, bigger inlet valves, a higher compression ratio, four wider-

throated 48IDF Weber carburettors with a larger airbox for better breathing, and a revised exhaust system. The result was a claimed 32 per cent increase in power, giving around 375bhp in the first cars, later rising to 400bhp+.

To keep it all in check, the suspension was made tauter, with adjustable Koni dampers, shorter springs and a beefier front anti-roll bar. Vented discs reduced brake fade, and fatter, lower-profile tyres provided extra grip and traction.

As magazine tests soon proved, the new Aston was every bit as quick as the more exotic supercar opposition, 0–60mph flashing up in a smidge over 5 seconds, the top speed being somewhere around 170mph. Today, too, a well-fettled Vantage is still an absolute event, with prodigious power and torque – second gear will pull all the way from 10mph to beyond the legal limit – and with a soundtrack to match.

It's not best on tightly twisting roads. With a 1,815-kg (2-ton) kerb weight to contain, even those beefier dampers and anti-roll bars can't defeat the laws of physics. But the rush of acceleration and adrenalin that floods in from 4,000rpm is intoxicating. Brutal, mechanical, uncompromising and thoroughly visceral – that's the Vantage.

1978
V8 Volante

More tourer than sports car, the V8 Volante is nevertheless an extremely seductive machine –
and a Bond car, too

I t's easy to underestimate the significance of the late-1970s V8 Volante. While the blissfully bonkers Lagonda Series 2 wedge grabbed the headlines, and the brutish Vantage became a poster car for a generation of schoolboys, it was orders for the Volante – particularly from the States – that pretty much kept the factory open through some of AML's most troubled times. While the Vantage had the magazine covers, the Volante quietly did the numbers.

No question, the Volante was a cruiser rather than a bruiser – the vast majority were ordered with Chrysler's Torqueflite three-speed auto, while the interior took Aston to new levels of walnut-trimmed opulence, and the extra weight took some of the edge off the performance. It's certainly hard to imagine Aston building anything quite as downright sybaritic as the V8 Volante today.

But can you think of anything better for cruising down to the French Riviera? There's something undeniably seductive about the Volante's blend of effortless urge, handsome hand-built body, sumptuous seating for four, and the ability to convert to open-air motoring at the push of a button.

Aston Martin stalwart Harold Beach was responsible for styling and engineering the conversion from coupé to drophead, and the crisp lines looked undeniably good, hood up or down. The hood mechanism nibbled into the rear-seat accommodation, though there were still four genuinely useable chairs, and the boot was smaller, too – though Aston thoughtfully provided fitted luggage as an optional extra.

Despite a steep asking price – £33,864/$72,000 when the standard coupé was £24,000/$43,200 – the Volante was an instant sales success, soon accounting for 75 per cent of production and helping to take Aston Martin back into the black.

In 1986 a Vantage Volante joined the range, distinguished by extended wheel arches and sill skirts. One famous customer of Aston Martin, Prince Charles, requested his with standard bodywork, and several more of these 'Prince of Wales' spec cars were also produced. Another Volante driver was 007 himself, with Aston boss Victor Gauntlett's own V8 Volante featuring briefly in the Dalton-era Bond film *The Living Daylights*.

SPECIFICATIONS

Years produced: 1978–89 **Engine:** V8, 5,340cc **Max power:** c.300bhp @ 6,000rpm
Max torque: c.300lb ft @ 5,000rpm **0–60mph:** c.7.0sec **Max speed:** 150mph
Price: £33,864/$72,000 new in 1979, £200,000+/$248,850+ today

1980

Bulldog

With its gullwing doors, twin-turbo V8 and 200mph+ top speed, the Bulldog was to be Aston's first hypercar.

Only one was ever built

SPECIFICATIONS

Years produced: 1980 **Engine:** V8, 5,340cc, twin-turbo **Max power:** 650bhp @ 6,500rpm
Max torque: 550lb ft @ 4,500rpm **0–60mph:** 4.5sec (est) **Max speed:** 200mph+
Price: £130,000/$317,200 new in 1981, £1 million+/$1.24 million (est) today

This was to be Aston Martin's answer to cars like the Lamborghini Countach – but even faster and more outrageous. William Towns' Lagonda Series 2 wedge had wowed the press and public, and now Towns was tasked with penning a mid-engined supercar. The results took the Lagonda's simple, angular, almost architectural forms to their ultimate expression. Engineering director Mike Loasby sketched the mechanical layout: a beefy tubular steel chassis supporting the suspension and cradling the familiar 5.3-litre Aston V8, but now positioned behind the driver, with the gearbox behind that.

Work began in 1977 but it didn't progress very far. Loasby left to join DeLorean, and Aston's management was preoccupied with the Lagonda. In early 1979, however, with Lagonda production finally under way, thoughts returned to the hypercar project.

With a target speed in excess of 200mph, turbocharging was the obvious way to extract sufficient power, and the team went for a brace of Garrett AiResearch T04B blowers, with Bosch fuel injection. On the dyno, this explosive cocktail eventually produced over 700bhp, though Aston quoted 650bhp for the finished car. The gearbox that sat behind was a ZF five-speed manual, while suspension was by double wishbones at the front and Aston's traditional de Dion axle at the rear.

The finished car was vast: 472cm (15ft 6in) long, well over 183cm (6ft) wide and just 109cm (3ft 7in) tall. The tyres were Pirelli P7s – massively wide 345/55s at the rear, just like the Countach's – and the brakes were vented and grooved 11½-inch (29.2-cm) iron discs with four-piston callipers – the sort of brakes that were then the preserve of CanAm sportscars.

So just how fast was it? It recorded 192mph at MIRA (the Motor Industry Research Association test track) and there were plans to take it to VW's Ehra-Lessien test track where it was expected to exceed 200mph – and would have been the first road-going supercar to do so. It wasn't to be. When it came to the crunch, Aston just didn't have the resources to put its supercar into production. So, instead, Bulldog took on a role as a showcase for the company's engineering talents.

Development engineer Keith Martin clocked up several thousand miles in the car during 1980. 'It was a delight to drive,' he recalls. 'And extremely quick, obviously, but not in a scary way. There wasn't the delay then the sudden kick you get with smaller turbocharged engines. The power just kept coming. And the sound was very much V8, but very loud, even when we fitted silencers. You could pootle around in traffic and on the M1 at 2000rpm in 5th at 70mph. On the test track, you'd be changing gear from third into fourth at 170mph with another gear to go!'

1982
Nimrod

In the early 1980s, Aston Martin made a bold return to Le Mans. The car was the V8-engined Nimrod.

The aim, outright victory...

SPECIFICATIONS

Years produced: 1982–84 **Engine:** V8, 5,340cc
Max power: 540bhp @ 6,250rpm **Max torque:** 440lb ft @ 5,000rpm **0–60mph:** n/a
Max speed: 213mph **Price:** n/a

N imrod was the brainchild of Aston Martin dealer and racer Robin Hamilton. In the late 1970s he'd flown the flag at Le Mans with a much-modified Aston V8 coupé, the RHAM/1, but that car was never going to be a challenger for outright honours. What was needed was a clean-sheet, mid-engined sports prototype for the new Group C category. So Hamilton took the momentous – some might even say foolhardy – decision to form an all-new team and commission a purpose-built racing car. Start-up investment came from Hamilton (reportedly to the tune of £125,000/$218,750), matched by AML chairman Victor Gauntlett on condition that the team used Aston Martin V8 race engines. The design of the car was entrusted to Eric Broadley – he of Lola T70 and Ford GT40 fame. And so the Aston Martin Nimrod programme was born.

The story of the Nimrod is a classic tale of British pluck. Under-resourced compared with the big factory effort from Porsche, the prospect of a brave independent British team, powered by an Aston engine, whipped up considerable patriotic fervour. The NRA/C2 featured an aluminium monocoque with GRP body panels, helping to keep the weight down to around 1,000kg (1.1 tons). The V8 produced around 540bhp and top speed was measured at 213mph.

For the 1982 Le Mans, there were in fact two teams running: the factory-backed Nimrod Racing effort, which numbered Tiff Needell among the drivers, and a privateer team funded by Aston-mad aristocrat Viscount Downe and run by specialist Richard Williams, who drafted in Ray Mallock to drive and help develop the car.

The Nimrod Racing car was running in the top ten in the early stages, until Needell had a big crash at near 200mph after the rear bodywork worked loose. The Viscount Downe car had better luck, running as high as third at around 3am before burnt-out valves slowly dropped them down the order to finish a highly creditable seventh overall.

For 1983, the Viscount Downe squad developed the car as the NRA/C2B, which now featured far prettier bodywork and more effective aerodynamics, but it was plagued by bad luck and unreliability. Unfortunately, the Nimrod's lasting Le Mans legacy is a monumental accident involving both cars entered for the 1984 race. Miraculously, both drivers survived, but the dream was dead. Nimrod had run its last Le Mans.

SPECIFICATIONS

Years produced: 1986–89 **Engine:** V8, 5,340cc **Max power:** 432bhp @ 6,250rpm
Max torque: 400lb ft @ 5,000rpm **0–60mph:** 4.8sec **Max speed:** 186mph
Price: £87,000 new in 1986 (not sold in the US), £250,000+/$311,050 today

1986
V8 Zagato

Twenty-five years after Aston Martin's original collaboration with Zagato on the DB4 GT, the relationship was rekindled. The result was startling

I **n the mid-1980s** interest from wealthy collectors for super-exotic low-volume supercars surged, and chairman Victor Gauntlett decided Aston should have its own slice of this lucrative pie. Looking back through the company history, he seized on the 1961 DB4 GT Zagato as the inspiration for an ultra-collectable, high-end Aston.

It's fair to say the new collaboration was a product of Zagato's punk era, an iconoclastic design that aroused powerful and divergent emotions. It's more than 30 years since it first rocked us on our heels, and while it retains the power to shock, it's now possible to appreciate just how successful the transformation was from V8 Vantage to V8 Vantage Zagato.

Some 17cm (6½in) shorter and 200kg (440lb) lighter than the donor car, it was Aston's first two-seater since the DB4 GT. With flush-fitting glass, stubby overhangs and a snortier, 432bhp version of the potent 5.3-litre V8, giving a top speed in excess of 180mph and a 0–60mph time of less than 5 seconds, it was one of the fastest and most accelerative cars in the world. Aston announced just 50 were to be built, and all were snapped up in hours of the programme being revealed.

It was quite common for Zagato owners to go for R S Williams' 6.3-litre conversion, less so the full-on, near-600bhp, 7.0-litre V8 found in the nose of E607 KYH (illustrated). Ahead of you sits that mountainous bonnet bulge (necessary to clear the airbox for the Weber 48 IDA carburettors beneath). In your peripheral vision you'll catch glimpses of the side windows, bisected by funky fenestration that allows one section to be lowered and raised within the main pane of glass. It has your pulse quickening even before you've turned a wheel.

The Zagato is so much more wieldy, so much more communicative than a regular V8 Vantage, with a tremendous sense of connection to the car and the road surface itself. It feels alive and hungry – and effortlessly fast, modest throttle openings really punching you down the road.

It handles, too, thanks to a responsive front end and a good balance of grip front to rear. Of course, you can sense the tail is willing to do the throttle's bidding. What's most impressive is that even when fitted with the 7-litre V8, the engine doesn't overwhelm the car – testament to the inherent balance and ability of the chassis.

1987
V8 Zagato Volante

With the Zagato coupé an instant sellout, Aston Martin aimed to repeat the dose with a soft-top version

SPECIFICATIONS

Years produced: 1987–89 **Engine:** V8, 5,340cc **Max power:** 432bhp @ 6,250rpm (Vantage spec)
Max torque: 400lb ft @ 5,000rpm **0–60mph:** c.5.0sec **Max speed:** c.180mph
Price: c.£90,000 new in 1987 (not available in the US), £250,000+/$311,050+ today

F ollowing the commercial success of the V8 Zagato coupé, Aston chairman Victor Gauntlett announced a run of 25 Volante versions. However, to keep the coupé buyers sweet, it was declared that the convertibles would have the less powerful fuel-injected V8 engine (though six of them – including the one in the photos here – were taken straight back to the factory and uprated to Vantage spec!). Again, demand was high and the eventual run of Volantes totalled 37.

Compared with the coupé, the V8 Zagato Volante looks rather genteel. Losing that turret top and glasshouse robs it of two unique and distinctive features, but it still has undeniable presence, especially when it's to Vantage specification, with the huge bonnet bulge to clear the stack of bored-out Weber carbs. By comparison, the fuel-injected cars had a flat bonnet that looked neater but rather emasculated, and most had curious headlight covers resembling the lid of a roll-top desk! Very Zagato…

So the Zagato Volante is a well-proportioned and surprisingly understated car that gives a genuinely beguiling driving experience. Quick, too, but far less combative than the war-like 7.0-litre coupé on the previous pages. The power delivery is sweeter, its responses slightly softer and the soundtrack steely but with a suggestion of mellowness and musicality.

It's an impressive and enjoyable car to drive but, to the hardcore Aston Martin enthusiast, Zagatos are meant to be athletic, shrink-to-fit coupés, so while it's possible to appreciate the Volante's broad appeal, the hardcore coupé is the car that most would always yearn to drive. Especially in a 7.0-litre spec!

Incidentally, while the V8 Zagato wasn't intended as a racing car, a handful of coupés – including one famously owned by Aston fan Rowan Atkinson – have been raced at Aston Martin Owners Club events in recent years.

1988
AMR1

After the Nimrod adventure, Le Mans was unfinished business for Victor Gauntlett and Aston Martin. In 1989, they were back again, with the awesome AMR1

Despite the ultimate disappointments of the Nimrod programme, Victor Gauntlett and Aston Martin co-owner Peter Livanos always wanted to return to Le Mans, and in late 1987 a new company, Proteus Technology, was formed with Richard Williams as MD and Ray Mallock as engineering director. Their target was the 1989 Le Mans 24 Hours, and they had an innovative designer, Max Bostrom, to shape the new contender.

AMR1 had one of the earliest all-carbon monocoques, with the roof and rollover structure built into the main body of the tub, but the innovation didn't stop there. It had its complete drivetrain canted at 7 degrees to clean the aero profile and allow a very wide venturi underbody; the gear cluster was ahead of the rear axle centre-line to improve weight distribution, and the car's aero performance over the Nimrod was almost beyond compare. The cutouts behind the front wheels were crucial, sucking air through and allowing the team to tune the front downforce. With a new 6-litre version of the V8 and a Reeves Callaway-developed four-valve head producing around 670bhp, the lighter, more slippery AMR1 with strong ground effects seemed a serious contender.

However, not all was rosy. With development running late, the AMR1 missed the first round of the championship.

Even more of an issue was that the rear-mounted radiators gave too much drag – hardly ideal for Le Mans. The 1989 race was the last to use the full Mulsanne, and the turbocharged Sauber Mercedes C9s were hitting an incredible 248mph. The AMR1's drag issues were stark – it could only manage around 217mph. AMR1/03 retired with engine failure but AMR1/01 was 11th in what was only the car's second race.

Away from Le Mans, the car's potential started to reveal itself. For the next round at Brands Hatch, they arrived with a new, lighter chassis, AMR1/04, and scored a competitive fourth. By the season's final round, a new iteration, AMR1/05 (pictured), had been lightened further and fitted with a new 6.3-litre engine with 740bhp. Furthermore, AMR2 was on the way with much reduced drag, helped by repositioning the radiators to the conventional location. Le Mans in 1990 was looking very exciting indeed. Then the rules changed.

The success of Group C meant Bernie Ecclestone saw it as a threat to F1, and the rules were changed overnight. Now you had to use a 3.5-litre F1-type engine. Ford had recently bought both Aston Martin and Jaguar and decided it would be Jaguar's Group C programme that would get Cosworth's 3.5-litre V8. Just like that, Proteus Technology was wound up and Aston's Group C adventure was over.

SPECIFICATIONS

Years produced: 1988–89 **Engine:** V8, 6,300cc
Max power: 740bhp @ 7,200rpm **Max torque:** 563lb ft @ 5,000rpm **0–60mph:** n/a
Max speed: c.220mph **Price:** n/a

1989

Virage

The classic V8 range was finally replaced in 1989. With a completely new shape and an updated V8 engine, the Virage was a fresh start

Looking back at early press reports on the Virage, you can't help but be struck by how effusive they were. The new, lightweight rear suspension, the updated V8 engine with its four-valve heads and state-of-the-art electronic fuel injection, and especially the smooth new bodywork by John Heffernan and Ken Greenley were all widely applauded. Even the faintly ludicrous list price – £129,000/$212,850 at launch, the equivalent to roughly a quarter of a million pounds/$311,175 today – seems to have been swallowed with barely a raised eyebrow. Well, these were the heady late 1980s…

It wasn't long before the initial gloss wore off. As the market turned, sales slowed. The Virage's looks didn't date well either, and when the wide-bodied 6.3-litre version appeared, the standard car looked distinctly underwhelming. For years, the Virage became one of the least-loved of the Aston family.

And yet… people are now warming to the Virage all over again. It is, after all, a proper, hand-built, aluminium-bodied, Marek-V8-engined Aston Martin. So how exactly does it feel to drive today?

Despite the portly 1,790-kg (1.97-ton) kerb weight, Aston claimed it would leap to 60mph in 6 seconds, but that was with the five-speed manual gearbox; many, like the car here, had the venerable three-speed Chrysler Torqueflite auto, and it really doesn't feel that quick. But it does have plenty of character.

Pull open the door and the smell of rich leather oozes out to meet you. And when you're perched high in the seat, surveying that vast expanse of aluminium bonnet, the Virage feels pretty special. Churn the V8 to life and the rich, bassy tones that wash back into the cabin confirm as much.

The three-speed auto is pretty clunky, but there's something quite enticing about how it thuds into 'D', the whole car straining to get going. Roll away on the easy-going torque, though, and the Virage doesn't feel that keen on doing much of anything. Initially, in fact, it feels imprecise and woolly, and despite a lot of noise, there's not much in the way of acceleration.

But with miles come signs of life. It takes quite a bit of steering lock to get through the flex in those 255/60 R16 Avon Turbospeed tyres and for the soft-edged suspension to load up, but as soon as the platform is sufficiently stable, the light rack weights up beautifully and every small input has an accurate and meaningful effect. It's as though the Virage's torpor is shaken off and the sports car – well, maybe sports GT – beneath reveals itself.

SPECIFICATIONS

Years produced: 1989–96 **Engine:** V8, 5,340cc **Max power:** 330bhp @ 6,000rpm
Max torque: 350lb ft @ 3,700rpm **0–60mph:** 6.0sec **Max speed:** 155mph
Price: £129,000/$212,850 new in 1989, £40,000+/$49,750 today

SPECIFICATIONS

Years produced: 1992–93 **Engine:** V8, 6,347cc **Max power:** 465bhp @ 6,000rpm
Max torque: 460lb ft @ 5,800rpm **0–60mph:** 5.5sec **Max speed:** 174mph
Price: £189,418 new in 1992 (not available in the US), £60,000+/$74,650+ today

1992
Virage 6.3

When Virage sales slowed, Aston Martin's proud engineers soon found ways to improve upon the rather meek standard car

O ver a period of just four years, the Virage would morph from tame GT to thundering twin-supercharged supercar, with attitude and muscle to strike fear into the hearts of the best from Italy and Germany. Aston Martin's grit, ingenuity, resourcefulness and wicked sense of humour were all bound up in that journey from Virage to Vantage. And nowhere was that more in evidence than with the intriguing wide-body Virage 6.3 developed by the Customer Service Division at Newport Pagnell, or Works, as it's better known.

It seems the guys at Works recognized the potential lost somewhere beneath the soft suspension and emissions equipment and decided to give the Virage a serious shot in the arm. The result was the Virage 6.3, a complete upgrade package launched in 1992 that included the obvious displacement increase, flared wheel arches to accommodate new wheels, tyres and much more convincing AP Racing brakes, new springs and dampers… in a nutshell, the full, ahem, Works.

The package gave the Virage a much more fulsome 465bhp at 6,000rpm (from 1993, a high-lift cam increased that again to 500bhp) and 460lb ft at 5,800rpm, and cost more than £50,000 on top of the c.£135,000 Virage. Customers lapped it up.

It looks the business. Isn't it amazing what a set of wide wheel arches and bigger wheels can do? From limp and almost apologetic, the Virage suddenly looks cartoonishly aggressive. And when the 6,347cc motor fires up with a dirty great bellow, the wildlife runs for cover. It's hard to believe the Virage spawned this monster just three years into its life.

The steering is really heavy for a power-assisted setup but all of the slack is gone and the suspension, which is so much firmer and more controlled, ensures the big car changes direction much more cleanly. So the Virage now feels leaner, and the V8 – even if still hampered by that three-speed auto – feels maybe 2 litres bigger and brawnier. It has the relentless pull that only comes with big capacity and natural aspiration. The noise is deeper and harder-edged, too.

This is how Aston's engineers always wanted the Virage to be. The grandly named 'Group C' AP Racing brakes are also a vast improvement. They were the first anti-lock brakes offered on any Aston, and the added bite and solid pedal feel are a great reassurance. Whether going fast or slowing down, the 6.3 is just more of an event.

SPECIFICATIONS (V550)

Years produced: 1993–2000 **Engine:** V8, 5,340cc, twin superchargers **Max power:** 550bhp @ 6,500rpm
Max torque: 550lb ft @ 4,000rpm **0–60mph:** 4.6sec **Max speed:** 186mph
Price: £177,600 new in 1993 (not available in the US), £175,000+/$217,900+ today

1993
Vantage V550/V600

The 6.3 Works conversion had whetted appetites for a faster Virage, and in 1993 Aston Martin finally unleashed the mighty Vantage

W hile Virage customers were upgrading to a 6.3-litre spec, a new and even more exciting development was going on behind the scenes. At the Birmingham motor show in September 1992, Aston Martin showed the Vantage. Every panel, save the roof and door skins, was new; in place of 16-inch wheels were gorgeous 18s wrapped in 285/45 ZR18 tyres; the AP Racing 350mm four-piston brakes with Bosch ABS were carried over from the 6.3; and with six headlights set behind glass, gaping air intakes and a bulging bonnet cut with cooling vents, the Vantage looked the business.

Under that fabulously dramatic bonnet was something pretty special, too. The old 5.3-litre V8 was given a new lease of life with the addition of two Eaton superchargers. The Vantage might weigh 1,920kg (2.12 tons) but, with 550bhp at 6,500rpm and a storming 550lb ft at 4,000rpm, it hardly seemed to matter. Driving through a six-speed manual gearbox (another first for Aston) the Vantage was good for 186mph and 0–60mph in 4.6 seconds.

Despite losing a litre of swept capacity to the 6.3, the V8 engine sounds unmistakably huge, the fast, howling idle enough to rattle bones. Compared with the 6.3, some of that car's heft has been dialled out of the steering, while the suspension feels a little more supple but also even more responsive… If the 6.3 car feels like a skunkworks hot rod, the Vantage is more polished, its talents running deeper.

So when you're going slowly, the Vantage is more relaxing, each control weight blended seamlessly with the next, the steering and suspension working in harmony. However, once you've squeezed the throttle to its stop and felt that mighty engine fling this huge car up the road, you don't care too much about going slowly. The Vantage can light up its rear tyres at 70mph! So you're always thinking about when you might unleash it, reading the road and listening to signals coming through the steering and seat to determine how those wide tyres are coping with the forces acting on them.

There was even more to come. In 1998, the V600 with 600bhp and 600lb ft became the world's most powerful production car. It was only made for a few years before the EU legislated it off the road, but, while it roamed the earth, there was nothing, absolutely nothing, quite like the supercharged Vantage, the 'roariest' and greatest dinosaur of all time.

DB7

For seven decades, Aston Martin built cars in tiny numbers and struggled to stay solvent.

With the DB7, everything changed

SPECIFICATIONS

Years produced: 1994–99 **Engine:** In-line 6-cylinder, 3,239cc **Max power:** 335bhp @ 5,750rpm
Max torque: 361lb ft @ 3,000rpm **0–60mph:** 5.8sec **Max speed:** 157mph
Price: £78,500/$140,000 new in 1994, £25,000+/$37,000+ today

When DB7 production finally ended in 2004, just over 7,000 examples had been built, which, at that point in time, was more than every other car Aston Martin had built in its entire history. The DB7 – both the original six-cylinder car and the V12-engined Vantage that came in 1999 – was without doubt a game-changer. Not only did it secure the marque's future but it proved Aston Martin could build cars in much greater numbers without diluting their desirability. And yet, compared with the Gaydon-era cars, these cars are still pretty exclusive machines and, for many people, the perfect 'first Aston Martin'.

In contrast with today's more muscular, chiselled Astons, the DB7's lines are softer and more elegant. Not exactly feminine but lithe. Inside, the cockpit is dominated by the plump seats and acres of leather. It feels good to slip behind the wheel, even if you do sit a little bit higher than you'd like. Reassuringly, the view through the windscreen, and in your peripheral vision, delivers the sense of being in something special, despite the switchgear and air vents famously sourced from a Ford parts bin.

The 3.2-litre six-cylinder supercharged engine looks like a big old lump when you lift the bonnet, but it sounds sweet enough when you fire it up. It doesn't do the whole 'look at me!' fanfare of recent Astons, but it makes a pleasingly brassy kerfuffle before settling into a rich, burbling idle.

Back in 1994, the straight-six's outputs weren't too shabby, the peaks of 335bhp and 361lb ft of torque endowing the 1,700-kg (1.87-ton) coupé with brisk, if not benchmark-setting, performance: 0–60mph in under 6 seconds and a top speed of 157mph. Twenty-odd years later, it's not exactly a fireball; if it's an auto, it's not even modern hot-hatch quick. But, once out onto faster roads, the DB7 finds a satisfying flow as the supple, touring-biased suspension soaks up the undulations and surface imperfections.

The handling balance is nicely neutral, with decent grip levels and plenty of traction, while the steering is responsive without being too alert. It's a car that prefers to hit its stride and stay there, rather than sprinting between corners then standing on its nose, but that's in keeping with its refined GT role. If you wanted more, Aston Martin was soon to deliver it…

SPECIFICATIONS

Years produced: 1996–99 **Engine:** V8, 5,340cc **Max power:** 354bhp @ 6,000rpm
Max torque: 368lb ft @ 4,300rpm **0–60mph:** 5.9sec **Max speed:** 155mph
Price: £139,500 new in 1993 (not available in the US), £60,000+/$74,650 today

1996
V8 Coupé

The basic Virage recipe, updated and refined, with a dash of big brother Vantage's square-jawed aggression

With sales of the standard Virage having run out of steam by the mid-1990s, Aston Martin relaunched the model as the V8 Coupé. This was Aston's Vantage-lite, sans superchargers, big brakes and wilder body modifications, but featuring revised bodywork inspired by its big brother, including its faired-in headlamps and four round tail-lights.

While it was an unvarnished attempt to garner sales of the slow-selling Virage/Vantage range, it was a far better car than the original Virage, gaining all the body, engine and weight-saving improvements of the supercharged cars. Power was slightly up on the original Virage, too, the acceleration slightly sharper. Sales were, however, glacially slow. In three years, just 101 Coupés and 63 Volante soft-top versions were sold.

Most of the 101 made were fitted with Chrysler's Torqueflite four-speed automatic, which didn't help the sporting image. Neither, of course, did any performance comparisons with the supercharged cars. With a top speed of 155mph, while the V600 was reported to have hit 200mph, and a 0–60mph time of 5.9 seconds against the V600's 3.9 seconds, it's hardly slow; it's just that the V600 is, well, epic.

By contrast with the supercharged cars, the V8 Coupé is a touch softer, with more movement in the rear suspension. You need to use the engine's revs, and with 1,500rpm between each gear change, it can feel a little hectic. It's reasonably refined, though there's a bit of wind bluster around the wing mirrors and screen at highway speeds. And, despite a Sport button that doesn't appear to do anything much, it's fast enough in its way – best on a sweeping major road with a good surface.

The Coupé is a proper GT in that respect and, while it doesn't have the all-out grunt of the supercharged cars, its lower price and much lower running costs, unstressed driveline, (relative) simplicity and brisk performance make it a companionable thing to drive. It really needs the manual transmission to make the most of the engine's torque, but manual Coupés are super-rare, with possibly only two production cars in existence.

1999
DB7 Vantage

The Vantage version of the DB7 saw the first appearance of a brand-new V12 engine.

It transformed the baby Aston into a junior supercar

Y ou need only lift the bonnet of the Vantage to appreciate the extraordinary metamorphosis the DB7 went through in its ten years of production. In place of the oblong cam-cover of the supercharged straight-six is the sensational-looking 5.9-litre V12, its rib-like inlet tracts filling the engine bay to the brim. This Cosworth-developed engine would go on to power a whole generation of Astons. With 420bhp and 400lb ft of torque, it gave the DB7 performance to rival a contemporary Ferrari 360 Modena, with 0–60mph in under 5 seconds and a top speed on the far side of 180mph.

Best of the lot was the GT model that came right at the end of the run. Of the 4,500 or so V12-engined DB7s built, just 191 were GTs (or the GTA auto version). As the ultimate series-production evolution of the DB7 Vantage, the GT gained 15bhp and 10lb ft over the regular V12-engined car, power and torque rising to 435bhp and 410lb ft, and the engine breathing more freely – and exuberantly! – through a sports exhaust.

Both chassis and aerodynamics were significantly improved, the former increasing in stiffness by 20 per cent, the latter reducing lift by almost 50 per cent. The six-speed manual transmission benefited from a quick-shift mechanism and a shorter final drive to boost in-gear acceleration. Top speed

remained unchanged from the regular Vantage at 185mph. It was – and is – a very serious, and seriously desirable, machine.

Pushing the big red illuminated 'Engine Start' button is a nice ritual, the generous punch of revs and decibels equally evocative. The clutch is weighty and has a long travel; the gear lever, too, has a satisfying heft. As you smoothly introduce the clutch plate to the flywheel, you're immediately struck by how much more potent the V12 feels than the in-line six – certainly more than even the quoted 100bhp and 50lb ft would have you believe.

It's a more precise, intense, sporty experience in every respect, but there's a residual mellowness and maturity that makes for a seductive combination of pace and poise, and one that's endlessly enjoyable to access, whether you're on a fast, open road or one that allows you to feel the full force of that epic engine in the lower gears.

Just one word of warning. Because it's more lively, you need to be mindful of what's at the command of your right foot. There is traction control, but the GT's tail will step out of line before it has you tightly in its grasp. Show it respect, though, and the GT is a proper drivers' Aston, and a fitting final fling for such a significant model.

SPECIFICATIONS

Years produced: 1999–2004 **Engine:** V12, 5,935cc **Max power:** 420bhp @ 6,000rpm (GT 435bhp)
Max torque: 400lb ft @ 5,000rpm (GT 410lb ft) **0–60mph:** 4.9sec **Max speed:** 185mph
Price: £92,500/$143,000 new in 2000, £30,000+/$37,350+ (GT £50,000+/$45,000) today

ASTONS IN MOTORSPORT

Racing has been in Aston Martin's blood since the very beginning, with Le Mans in particular proving an irresistible challenge

A ston Martin: even the name has its roots embedded in motorsport. Aston Hill in Buckinghamshire was the scene of some of Lionel Martin's earliest successes in competitive hill-climbing, and when Martin and business partner Robert Bamford were weighing up potential names for their new sports car in 1914, they decided that 'Aston Martin' had a ring to it. How right they were…

Their pioneering exploits were put on hold as conflict gripped Europe and engineers and factories were conscripted for the war effort, but in 1919 they reassembled their small team. The following year, the unflatteringly named Coal Scuttle made the marque's first appearance on the famous banked corners of the Brooklands track in Surrey, Lionel Martin himself taking three second places at the Junior Car Club May Meeting.

Further eye-catching successes followed, and in 1921 a new car, named Bunny, finished a creditable fifth in the Voiturette Grand Prix at Le Mans. The next year, Bunny would break no fewer than ten world and 22 'light car' records during a 16-hour 20-minute endurance marathon at Brooklands, covering 1,200 miles at an average of 76mph. The Aston Martin name was starting to get noticed…

Alas, the business wasn't performing as well as the cars, and the company went into receivership in 1925. But from its ashes rose a new Aston Martin company in 1926, led by racer and engineer Augustus Cesare 'Bert' Bertelli. Inevitably, Bertelli wanted to go racing, and in 1928 Aston began its long – and often torrid – affair with the Le Mans 24 Hours. Two 'team cars' with dry-sump versions of the new 1,492cc OHC engine were entered, and, while both retired, Aston Martin won a special prize for fastest 1.5-litre car over the first 20 laps.

Le Mans start: Vantage GTE leads the GT field in the 2013 race

Carroll Shelby, David Brown and Jack Fairman aboard a DBR1

As the 1920s became the early 1930s, Astons continued to perform creditably at Brooklands and Le Mans. The best result yet came at the 1933 Le Mans, when Astons finished fifth and seventh overall and won their class, and the following year factory cars won the team prize in the Ulster Tourist Trophy. It was in their honour that the next generation of road-racers was named Ulster, and it was these cars that would head Aston Martin's presence in competition across Europe through the mid- and late 1930s, scoring numerous class wins in the hands of both works and privateer drivers. In 1935, Astons finished 1-4-5-6-7-8 in class at Le Mans, winning the prestigious Biennial Cup, the first car home also finishing third overall. It was the closest Aston had come to an overall win in the world's most famous endurance race – a dream that would become almost an obsession in the next chapter of Aston's motorsport story.

David Brown never made a secret of his ambition to win Le Mans outright. It was one of the things that drove him to buy Lagonda and, with it, the twin-cam straight-six engine that would – in various guises – power nearly all of Aston Martin's sports-racers for the next decade. That engine made its debut in one of three DB2s entered for the 1949 Le Mans and, though it failed in that race, the following year Aston was back with three six-cylinder cars and scored an impressive first and second in the 3-litre class and fifth and sixth overall. In 1951 they went even better, finishing third, fifth and seventh overall and taking the first three places in class.

By that time, Brown had hired Dr Robert Eberan von Eberhorst, the designer of the awesome prewar Auto Union 'Silver Arrows', to create a new sports-racer, the DB3. It wasn't a great success. Although the DB3 did record some decent results, most notably a win in the 1952 Goodwood Nine Hours, it was often off the pace of the (usually Ferrari and Jaguar) opposition. What was needed was a radical rethink, and it came in the exquisite shape of the DB3S, one of the true postwar greats. The

DB3S out-drags Jaguar D-type at Aintree in 1956

credit here belongs chiefly to Willie Watson, a fine engineer who worked wonders in turning the overweight, oversized and underpowered DB3 into the fantastically trim and effective DB3S that was to be competitive for a whole four seasons, from 1953 to 1956.

In the 3-litre class of the day, DB3Ss were nearly always the cars to beat – and on tracks with shorter straights than Le Mans they would often show the bigger-engined D-types and Ferraris a clean pair of heels, too. Not that their record at Le Mans was too shabby, finishing second overall in 1955, 1956 and 1958.

Yet outright victory in the 24 Hours still eluded Brown and Aston Martin. While the DB3S was a fine car, its road-car origins meant it was heavy compared with the Ferraris and Maseratis of the day. So when Le Mans announced an engine ceiling of 2.5 litres for 1956, that was the cue Aston needed to develop a completely bespoke racer from scratch. This car would be the DBR1, with its ultra-lightweight spaceframe chassis, rear-mounted gearbox, exotic alloy materials and super-sleek bodywork.

The DBR1 prototype ran strongly at Le Mans on its debut in 1956 before retiring after 21 hours. But though its pace was obvious, mechanical problems caused retirements in both 1957 and 1958.

In 1959, however, the stars finally aligned. Aston threw everything it had at that race, including three DBR1s. Stirling Moss set the early pace, but it was DBR1/2, driven by Carroll Shelby and Roy Salvadori, that took the flag amid great jubilation – and no little relief.

There was still the small matter of the World Sportscar Championship, which was left to Moss to clinch at Goodwood, and not before further drama, Aston famously setting fire to its leading car during a pit stop. One of the other DBR1 drivers, Graham Whitehead, withdrew his car to allow Aston to use his pit stall for DBR1/2, which

Roy Salvadori driving DBR1/2 to victory at Le Mans, 1959

Moss took over, catching and beating the Porsche and Ferrari threat. Victory gave Aston a total of 24 points against Ferrari's 22 and with them the championship. For David Brown, champagne never tasted better.

His goal achieved, Brown immediately announced the winding-up of the factory race programme, though in the years that followed support was often given to privateer teams. These included the Essex Racing Stable, which ran a number of Astons, including the gorgeous DB4 GT Zagato.

In 1962, however, under pressure from American dealers for a full-blown factory effort at Le Mans, Aston Martin returned with DP212, a modified DB4 GT with a 330bhp straight-six, de Dion rear suspension, and beautifully streamlined aluminium bodywork, the first of the so-called Project Cars. Despite taking an early lead, it retired after five hours with piston trouble.

For the following year's race, the theme was taken further with the even more exotic DP214 and 215, the latter setting a speed record for front-engined cars of 198.5mph. Alas, neither would finish the race, though Project 214s would come first and third in that year's Inter-Europa Cup at Monza.

Below: Project car DP212   Right: Jim Clark drifts a DB4 GT Zagato

122

With that, the factory once again bowed out of front-line motorsport, though in the late 1960s it did agree to supply its new V8 engine, still in the relatively early stages of development, to John Surtees' Lola-Aston project. Installed in the well-proven Lola T70 chassis, the V8 showed initial promise but both cars entered for the 1967 Le Mans retired with engine problems and the project folded soon after.

In the 1970s it was left to Aston dealer and racer Robin Hamilton to fly the flag with a much-modified (and eventually turbocharged) V8 coupé, officially called RHAM/1 but nicknamed The Muncher because of its insatiable appetite for brake discs. This outlandish creation confounded the sceptics by finishing third in class in the 1977 Le Mans, recording 188mph on the Mulsanne in the process.

But The Muncher was never going to win Le Mans outright and so, in the early 1980s, Hamilton put all his energies – and a fair bit of cash, too – into a full-on mid-engined sports-prototype for the new Group C category. The car was called the Nimrod, and Hamilton persuaded Aston boss Victor Gauntlett to match his investment, which Gauntlett agreed to do on condition that Nimrod Racing bought its Aston V8s from AML's Tickford engineering subsidiary.

Two cars entered the 1982 race. The factory-backed Nimrod Racing car ran in the top ten in the early stages until Tiff Needell had a monumental crash; the second car, entered by a privateer team backed by Viscount Downe, ran as high as third at one stage and finished the race a highly commendable seventh.

That was as good as it got for the Nimrod, but Gauntlett had had a taste of Le Mans, and in 1988 he instigated a new Group C car, the AMR1, with a new 6-litre version of the V8 engine, an all-carbon structure and sophisticated (for the day) ground-effect aerodynamics. It only competed at one Le Mans, in 1989, one car retiring with engine failure, the other finishing a middling 11th. Other results were more encouraging, including a strong fourth place at the 480km of Brands Hatch. But then the rules changed, making the big V8 engine obsolete, and with parent company Ford deciding to back Jaguar rather than Aston, the AMR1 project was wound up.

Below: 'The Muncher' at Le Mans

Right: Gauntlett, Hamilton and the Nimrod team

Lola-Aston DBR1-2 finished fourth at Le Mans in 2009

There then followed a long hiatus before, in 2004, Prodrive boss David Richards persuaded Aston CEO Ulrich Bez to get behind a new sports-car challenger in the shape of the DB9-derived DBR9, which would run in the popular GT1 category. The idea was to mirror how the DB3S had been sold and raced in the 1950s, some DBR9s being run by the newly formed Aston Martin Racing, others by privateers. In a long and successful racing career that lasted until 2011, the DBR9 would score numerous podiums – and all capped off with a return to Le Mans glory, with back-to-back wins in the GT1 class in 2007 and 2008.

Prodrive, in the guise of Aston Martin Racing, has gone on to develop a whole series of V8 Vantage-based GT racers, which in recent years have competed in the World Endurance Championship, the Blancpain GT3 series and a host of national GT series in the UK, Europe, the US and the Far East. The latest of these is the stunning

V8 Vantage GTE makes a pit stop at the 2013 24 Hours

DBR9 scored back-to-back wins in the GT1 class in 2007 and 2008

V8 Vantage GTE was a WEC title winner in 2016

V8 Vantage GTE, new for the 2016 season and proving a consistent front-runner in the World Endurance Championship.

Will an Aston ever again challenge for outright victory at Le Mans? In 2007, AMR instigated another joint Lola-Aston project, installing the DBR9's 6-litre V12 in the chassis of Lola's LMP1 car (Le Mans Prototype 1 being the top class in the Le Mans race series). The following year, a Lola-Aston B08/60 finished ninth overall at Le Mans, while its successor, the B09/60 (rather controversially renamed DBR1-2 to echo the 1959 Le Mans-winning car) achieved a laudable fourth place in the 2009 race.

Then, in 2011, AMR revealed a new Le Mans prototype, the AMR-One. But with no links to Aston Martin's road cars, or even previous racing cars – the engine was a downsized 2-litre turbo straight-six – enthusiasm for the project among Aston fans was lukewarm and the car itself underperformed. The project was canned the following year.

So, for now at least, attention is focused on the GT cars. But with the Adrian Newey-designed Valkerie hypercar on the distant horizon and the possibility of further Red Bull collaborations, you don't have to be too much of a dreamer to envisage a full assault on Le Mans somewhere down the line. Victory in the 24 Hours will always be the ultimate prize.

THE
MODERN
ERA

The Modern Era – Introduction

Ford money – and a bulldog spirit – had ensured Aston Martin's survival; now, on the cusp of a new millennium, it was about to enter its most successful era yet

Project Vantage, the concept car that would become the Vanquish, had been unveiled in 1998, but it wouldn't be until 2001 that the production-ready car would be launched. The delay was caused, at least in part, by another significant arrival – that of new chief executive Dr Ulrich Bez. The former Porsche product design boss wanted things to be done his way, and that included the new flagship.

Delayed or not, the Vanquish was a watershed for Aston Martin, effectively straddling the old and new eras. The last model built – largely by hand – at Newport Pagnell, it also saw Aston break new ground with an innovative extruded aluminium chassis, developed in conjunction with Lotus. This was the forerunner of what would become known as the VH platform – a way of spinning various models from the same basic structure and manufacturing process that would serve Aston for the next decade and beyond.

The first car to use the VH platform, and also the first to be built in the brand-new factory at Gaydon in Warwickshire and really the first new model of the modern Aston era, was the DB9. Here was a truly world-class product built using state-of-the-art production techniques, a car for which no allowances needed to be made.

The following year, 2005, Aston launched the V8 Vantage, an 'entry-level' Aston designed to lure a younger audience away from their Porsche 911s. It would go on to become the best-selling Aston of all time, with sales to date of around 20,000, and in turn spawn a Roadster version and, in 2009, the fabulous V12 Vantage.

The design studio at Gaydon

130

The last car to be built at Newport Pagnell was the Vanquish S

Meanwhile, the new flagship car, the DBS, made its debut alongside Daniel Craig as James Bond in *Casino Royale*. It was just like the old glory days. Confidence buoyed, in 2005 Dr Bez announced a return to the racetrack with the DB9-based DBR9. The programme would be run by the newly formed Aston Martin Racing, led by Prodrive boss David Richards, and the DBR9 would go on to win the GT1 class at Le Mans in 2007 and 2008.

David Richards was to play an even bigger part in the next chapter of the Aston story. Cash-strapped Ford was divesting itself of assets, and in 2007 Richards led a consortium to buy the company, becoming chairman himself while Ulrich Bez remained as CEO. The same year saw the last Vanquish roll off the production line at Newport Pagnell.

Gaydon-era Astons use a bonded aluminium platform

Within months the old factory site was flattened, though the old Works Service on the opposite side of Tickford Street would remain – and flourish.

More fabulous cars flowed from Gaydon, including the One-77 supercar (2009), V12 Zagato (2011) and a new Vanquish flagship (2012). There was the occasional misstep, too: retrimming a Toyota to sell as an Aston Martin (2010's Cygnet city car) didn't go down well with many enthusiasts.

As the economy contracted, sales slowed from their mid-2000s peak, but in 2013 Aston Martin was able to celebrate 100 years since its foundation with a year of memorable centenary celebrations, culminating in a spectacular timeline of 100 iconic models at Kensington Palace.

At the end of the centenary year, Ulrich Bez stood down as CEO and, soon after, David Richards relinquished the role of chairman as new investors came on board, including Daimler, with whom Aston Martin signed a technical partnership. In 2014 British-born, ex-Nissan high-flyer Andy Palmer took up the reins, telling the workforce: 'Together we will create the next generation of Aston Martins.'

The first of those new Astons, and the first fruit of the partnership with Daimler, was the DB11, launched in the summer of 2016. With a replacement for the Vantage range on the horizon and an extraordinary mid-engined hypercar in development, the future of this proud and special marque looks as exciting as it has ever done.

One-77's mighty 7.3-litre V12 engine

DB11 was the first fruit of Aston's 'second-century plan'

SPECIFICATIONS

Years produced: 2001–07 **Engine:** V12, 5,935cc **Max power:** 460bhp @ 6,500rpm
Max torque: 400lb ft @ 5,000rpm **0–60mph:** 5.0sec **Max speed:** 190mph
Price: £160,000/$228,000 new in 2001, £60,000+/$76,900+ today

2001
V12 Vanquish

This was the car that launched Aston Martin into the modern era, a radical departure from the old school and now a modern classic

W hat's in a name? If it happens to be Vanquish, then little short of everything, for rarely has a moniker made a more serious statement of intent. Such a provocative christening was fighting talk from Aston Martin, and nothing was held back in the efforts to deliver a fitting standard-bearer for the new millennium.

It didn't disappoint. Taking a bold step into the future without severing its ties with the past, the Vanquish was a radical departure that marked a pivotal phase in Aston Martin's modern history. More sophisticated than any Aston before it and dressed in a striking new suit to match, it made the critical shift from traditional hand-built methods to one where 21st-century technology – including a radical new bonded aluminium platform and a paddleshift gearbox – was the driving force. The result was a car that grabbed headlines, stole hearts and shook its rivals by the lapels.

Today, it remains one of Ian Callum's most inspired pieces of work. Those pure forms and chiselled lines somehow captured the essence of Aston Martin without plundering the marque's enviable back catalogue of curves, while details such as the ruthlessly slash-cut sills remain as striking now as they did in 2001.

The interior is prescient of the Gaydon-era cars we know today. You sit high in the car, perched on it rather than in it, but you soon forget this when you turn the ignition key and the big red 'Engine Start' switch illuminates on the dashboard. Give it a prod and a split-second of unmistakable starter-motor churn cedes to a brassy burst of engine revs that trumpets from the pair of slash-cut tailpipes. The sound quickly becomes an aural metaphor that defines your memories of the car: smooth, savage and still quite unique, even among the many other V12-engined Astons before and since this car was introduced.

Nudge the brake pedal, pull back on the right-hand paddle for first gear and – provided you don't have too much stop-start driving or low-speed shunting to do – the Vanquish pulls away cleanly. Downshifts are punchy and accompanied by a meaty flare of revs, but upshifts require a little patience and mechanical sympathy, a slight lift of the throttle smoothing things nicely. It never was a brilliant gearbox when new, and now it feels rather quaint, but so long as you're prepared to make allowances, it's far from the catastrophe you might fear and certainly doesn't get in the way of enjoying the car or accessing its performance.

With 460bhp and 400lb ft of torque, the 1,835-kg (2.02-ton) Vanquish is no slouch. Maximum power arrives at 6,500rpm, peak torque at 5,000rpm, so it likes to rev, but those numbers belie a car that can make majestic progress on partial throttle openings. Not that you'll want to restrict yourself to part-throttle, for the way it goes – and sounds – when the taps are fully opened confirms what it is that sets V12s apart from all other engines, and Aston Martins from all other cars. Who knows what sonic shenanigans take place within the Vanquish's pipework and silencer boxes (it was one of the first cars to have its sound carefully analysed and engineered), but the result is one of the finest exhaust notes you'll ever hear.

Chassis-wise, the Vanquish is a satisfying blend of pliancy and control. Its passive suspension (no electronic wizardry here) is soft-edged and works in harmony with the road, but rarely gets wrong-footed by its bumps, cambers or compressions. The steering has a lightness immediately around the straight-ahead, but once you've initiated your steering input, there's a beautiful weightiness and assured rate of response that immediately gives you confidence that the front end is keyed-in. Squeeze into the throttle's generous travel and the car remains wonderfully neutral, lateral forces distributed evenly front to rear for a great sense of poise and balance.

Driven with a little more aggression and commitment, the Vanquish's tail can be made to wag, but its quick wits and deep reserves of progressively delivered torque mean, so long as you're measured and confident, you can drive to, and eventually beyond, the adhesive limits of the rear tyres. Like all great, fast cars it still has a sharp set of teeth – especially on cold, wet roads – but it only ever bites if you provoke it. The electronic traction control tames the beast, but lacks the finesse and nuanced control of today's systems, so there will be times when you'll be tempted to switch it off. Pay it the respect any near-500bhp rear-wheel drive car deserves and you'll be fine, but take liberties and you'll need to be ready to answer the questions the Vanquish will ask.

SPECIFICATIONS

Years produced: 2003–04 **Engine:** V12, 5,935c **Max power:** 435bhp @ 6,000rpm
Max torque: 410lb ft @ 5,000rpm **0–60mph:** 4.8sec **Max speed:** 190mph
Price: £160,000 new in 2003 (not available in the US), £200,000+/$248,850 today

2003
DB7 Zagato

With familiar Zagato design cues and the drivetrain from the excellent DB7 GT,
the DB7 Zagato was another winning collaboration

Much like fine wines or whiskies, Zagato Astons seem to get better with age. The DB7 Zagato – just 99 of which were sold – never had the V8 Zagato's shock value, but that's largely because it followed in the V8's wake. It was also less of a stylistic departure from the regular production car: an evolution rather than a total reinvention.

But the Zagato elements are key. They include the double-bubble roof, leading into the deliciously curved rear window, and the oversize mouth with its chip-cutter grille – combined with a slightly shorter wheelbase, they give the comparatively polite DB7 some real attitude.

The interior is less impressive. Those Ford-sourced switches look a bit cheap and the instruments also seem a bit too mainstream for an 'exotic'. Those areas that Aston could influence, such as the wonderful aniline leather upholstery, lift the ambience and feel unmistakably special. Despite the lack of expensive detailing, it has that all-important sense of occasion, especially when you glance in the rear-view mirror and see the distortions generated by that undulating rear screen.

Powered by the GT's 435bhp version of the 5.9-litre V12, the DB7 Zagato sounds like it means business: big-hearted and potent. The six-speed manual gearbox has a weighty shift quality but a longish throw. The clutch requires modest effort. Thanks to the V12's abundant muscle and smooth manners, it makes assured, comfortable progress in that all-important phase when you begin to bond with the machine.

Explore more of the throttle's long travel and the DB7 Zagato reveals a satisfying blend of emphatic, any-revs response, rounded ride, measured steering and sure-footed balance. Wind it through the last 1,500rpm of its rev-range in the intermediate gears and it lunges between the corners with the kind of otherworldly shove that makes any V12-engined car so seductive to drive.

Where it scores over the DB7 GT is the increased agility you get from the shorter wheelbase. It's keener to peel into corners, sharper and more incisive when you ask it to make quick direction changes. There is traction control, but it's a far cry from today's sophisticated systems and can feel a bit clumsy and slow-witted when it does intervene. It can be disabled, but hooning really isn't the DB7 Zagato's style. Better to keep things smooth, get it settled into the corner then revel in the V12's huge spread of power and soaring soundtrack.

2003
DB AR1

The DB7 Zagato's roadster cousin isn't the most dynamic of Astons, but then it was aimed squarely at cruising and the American sunshine states

M uch like its name, the DB American Roadster 1, or DB AR1 for short, is something of a strange fish. Built only for the US after homologation issues prevented the DB7 Zagato from being sold Stateside, the AR1 borrowed heavily from the coupé's styling but applied it to the longer wheelbase of the standard DB7.

With no roof whatsoever, it was designed for a charmed life on the sunbaked West Coast – or, more likely, in the air-conditioned, dehumidified cocoons of wealthy collectors' garages. As a result, European enthusiasts regarded it somewhat sniffily, for it seemed to have been too compromised to be taken seriously.

Was that strictly fair? Looking at the DB AR1 alongside other Aston Zagatos, I think it probably is, though it does appear rather more graceful in the metal. The real problem is that, as with the V8 Zagato Volante, lopping the roof off seems to diminish its identity. This is even more marked in the case of the DB7 – losing such a pronounced double-bubble roof and beautifully sculpted rear window. That said, the DB AR1's double-cowl deck lid makes its own dramatic statement – and you're better able to admire that quilted leather interior.

It's incredibly rare to see a DB AR1 in the UK, and, as its styling and target market suggest, the driving experience is more boulevard than back road. The longer wheelbase makes it feel less dynamic than the coupé, which, in turn, means you feel less inclined to drive it with genuine commitment. It's a softer and more mellow machine, which, though not a crime, does seem at odds with what a Zagato should be. Whether this was the reason 'Zagato' was not included in the name has not been documented.

Of course, the obvious benefit of having no roof is your exposure to the elements. On a summer's day this would most certainly be a fantastic experience, not least because you are immersed so completely in the V12's sonorous exhaust note. And if the svelte AR1 is the least compelling of the Anglo-Italian collaborations, that only speaks volumes about the enduring magic of Aston Martin and Zagato's inspired – and inspirational – partnership.

SPECIFICATIONS

Years made: 2003–2004 **Engine:** V12, 5935c **Max power:** 435bhp @ 6000rpm
Max torque: 410lb ft @ 5000rpm **0–60mph:** 5.0sec **Top speed:** 170mph (est)
Price: c$250,000 new in 2003 (US only), £200,000/$248,850+ today

SPECIFICATIONS

Years produced: 2004–07 **Engine:** V12, 5,935cc **Max power:** 520bhp @ 7,000rpm
Max torque: 425lb ft @ 4,500rpm **0–60mph:** 4.9sec **Max speed:** c.200mph
Price: £174,000/$255,000 new in 2004, £150,000+/$105,900 today

2004
V12 Vanquish S

With more power, improved handling and aerodynamics, and numerous detail improvements, the 'S' was the Vanquish turned up to 11

When Aston introduced the Vanquish S in 2004, its charismatic flagship instantly joined the supercar greats. An increase in power from 460 to 520bhp and accompanying aerodynamic changes lifted the top speed to 200mph; reworked suspension tautened the handling; and there were worthwhile refinements to many other aspects of the car, including the paddleshift automated manual gearbox. It was a resounding success.

Today, a well-maintained S still feels deliciously fast and capable. On longer journeys, this consummate GT settles quickly into a beautifully relaxed lope. Despite weighing just over 2,000kg (2.2 tons), it feels remarkably light and easy to drive: the steering requires little effort and, even if you take it out of auto, the gear change is no more taxing than pulling a trigger. Yes, the single-clutch paddleshift gearbox is like dial-up versus fibre-optic when compared with current dual-clutch offerings, but it was improved throughout the life of the car and there's something quite enjoyable about judging the requisite amount to back out of the throttle to smooth an upshift.

Despite its 1,875-kg (2.06-ton) kerb weight, the Vanquish S likes to be hustled. The traction control is surprisingly relaxed, so you always have to be on your game, especially in the wet.

There is perhaps more roll in the suspension than you might initially expect, and those GT credentials mean it's no out-and-out sports car. Yet somehow the Vanquish always gives a wonderful feeling of connection to the road. There's a fantastic balance to the handling, too. Tackling a small sequence of corners where the road dips and crests as it turns right then left is the sort of thing that could tie such a big car in knots, but the S is just sublime.

There are three things in particular that make a Vanquish S so desirable today. First, there's the glorious sound of the V12 and, second, there's its appearance: few modern Astons can compete with the subtle muscularity of the original Vanquish. The way the metal skin looks like it has been pulled taut over shapes beneath is somehow more organic than anything that has worn the winged badge since.

Finally, there's the fact that it was the last car hand-built at Newport Pagnell. Many believe that photos shot on film have an indefinable quality that digital can never quite replicate, whatever the pixel count. Likewise, despite the undoubted accuracy and advantages of modern automated construction techniques, a car made by hand will always possess something a little bit extra…

2004
DB9

Only a car of rare beauty could replace the DB7, and the DB9, the first Aston to be built at Gaydon,

had both the looks and the ability to do so

SPECIFICATIONS

Years produced: 2004–12 (first generation) **Engine:** V12, 5,935cc **Max power:** 450bhp @ 6,000rpm
Max torque: 420lb ft @ 5,000rpm **0–60mph:** 4.9sec **Max speed:** 186mph
Price: £109,000/$155,000 new in 2004, £30,000+/$44,600+ today

he international launch of the DB9 in 2004 was held high in the Alpes-Maritimes, overlooking the French Riviera; the roads were fabulous and the car was completely seductive. This was the first taste of Gaydon-era Aston Martin and the innovative, all-aluminium VH platform, and it certainly didn't disappoint, putting the marque back on the map as builder of the world's most desirable GT cars.

Will this car's beauty ever fade? If anything, the DB9's svelte simplicity and inherent modesty become more compelling as the years pass. It's such an elegant car – especially in this lovely shade of California Sage Green – you can't help but feel the need to put on an expensive suit and drive to some suave European capital.

Things get even better when you grasp the pop-out handle and swing open the driver's door – these early DB9s are also blessed with a truly fabulous interior. The sculpted door cappings and the cascading swoop that forms the central 'waterfall', running from the dashboard down into the centre console, look absolutely stunning.

Available at launch only with the Touchtronic paddleshift torque-converter automatic transmission, Aston did subsequently offer the six-speed manual gearbox as well. Those cars are tremendous fun – especially when equipped with the optional Sport Pack – for they really bring out the DB9's sporting character. Unfortunately, they are also very rare. Don't be too downhearted, though, for the Touchtronic gearbox is a sublime partner to the 5.9-litre V12. If you intend

to use a DB9 in its classic role as a fast and effortless long-distance mile-eater, it's arguably the spec to have.

Dab the brake pedal, push the lovely glass starter button and smile as the engine growls into life. There's purpose in the exhaust note and potency in the way it makes its presence felt in the cockpit, but the DB9 stops short of being shouty. In fact it's the four-wheeled embodiment of the adage 'speak softly and carry a big stick'.

You have the choice of simply pressing D and letting the ZF transmission shuffle the deck of ratios for you, or pulling the paddles yourself. Elect to do the former and you're treated to that endlessly impressive delivery that's unique to big-capacity V12s. Never lazy, but never frantic, you luxuriate in the engine's any-revs tractability and thrill to the cultured, turbine-like hum that percolates into the cockpit

with modest throttle openings. Use the paddles and you feel more inclined to explore the V12's mighty range. Dig beyond the generous low- and mid-range torque and you discover substantial reserves of top-end power. It's too polite to really bare its teeth, but the way it snarls as you punch down straights and power through corners is inspiring to say the least.

Chassis-wise, early DB9s could be a mixed bag. The launch cars felt fabulous, but the first production examples could have a brittle edge to the ride. Later cars felt nicely pliant, but with an underlying tautness that's appropriate for what is a truly sporting luxury GT. Up the ante and you do begin to find the limits of the damping, but it doesn't lose its cool. As an all-round package, a first-generation DB9 is virtually irresistible.

2005
DBR9

Aston Martin roared back to winning ways at Le Mans with the magnificent DBR9,

this very car scoring back-to-back wins in the GT1 class

I t was David Richards, boss of Prodrive and soon to be boss of Aston Martin Racing, who recognized in the DB9 the basis for a contender in international sports-car racing, and in 2004 he persuaded Aston to lend its name and support to a new GT1 programme. The rest, as they say, is history. A debut win in the Sebring 12 Hours and consecutive GT1 class wins at Le Mans in 2007 and 2008 were just the biggest highlights in a racing career that only ended when the GT1 category was canned in 2011.

The DBR9 used the DB9's aluminium platform and V12 engine, but the rest was developed for racing. The bodywork was all carbon fibre, helping to keep the weight down to just 1,100kg (1.21 tons), which gave a power-to-weight ratio of 554bhp per ton. With six-speed sequential manual transmission, that was enough to blast it from 0–60mph in 3.4 seconds, while with Le Mans gearing it could top 200mph.

It was car 009 that took the famous win in 2007, and a year later it was 009 again, repainted in the iconic Gulf Oil livery, that repeated the dose. So a chance to get behind the wheel is a very, very special privilege.

By today's standards, the driving environment is somewhat old-school. An oversize sequential gear lever sprouts from the transmission tunnel, whereas today's cars have paddles. But there's nothing to date its performance. The DBR9 more than doubles the power-to-weight ratio of a DB9 road car and that stat doesn't begin to do its hair-prickling performance justice. Nor does it ready you for the intense, buzz-saw wail of the V12, the responsiveness of the controls or the mechanical and aerodynamic grip that, thanks to sticky Michelin slicks, huge wings and tarmac-sucking rear diffuser, will generate up to 3.0g of lateral load if you have the courage to carry the requisite corner speed.

A man who knows how that feels better than anyone is Darren Turner, a driver in both GT1 Le Mans wins. 'They were properly exciting things to race', he says. 'There's nothing quite like the sound or the delivery of a racing V12, and that Aston motor was very special. The aero and brakes were also mega, and the cars just looked so good on track. For me the DBR9 was a great car in a glorious era of GT racing.'

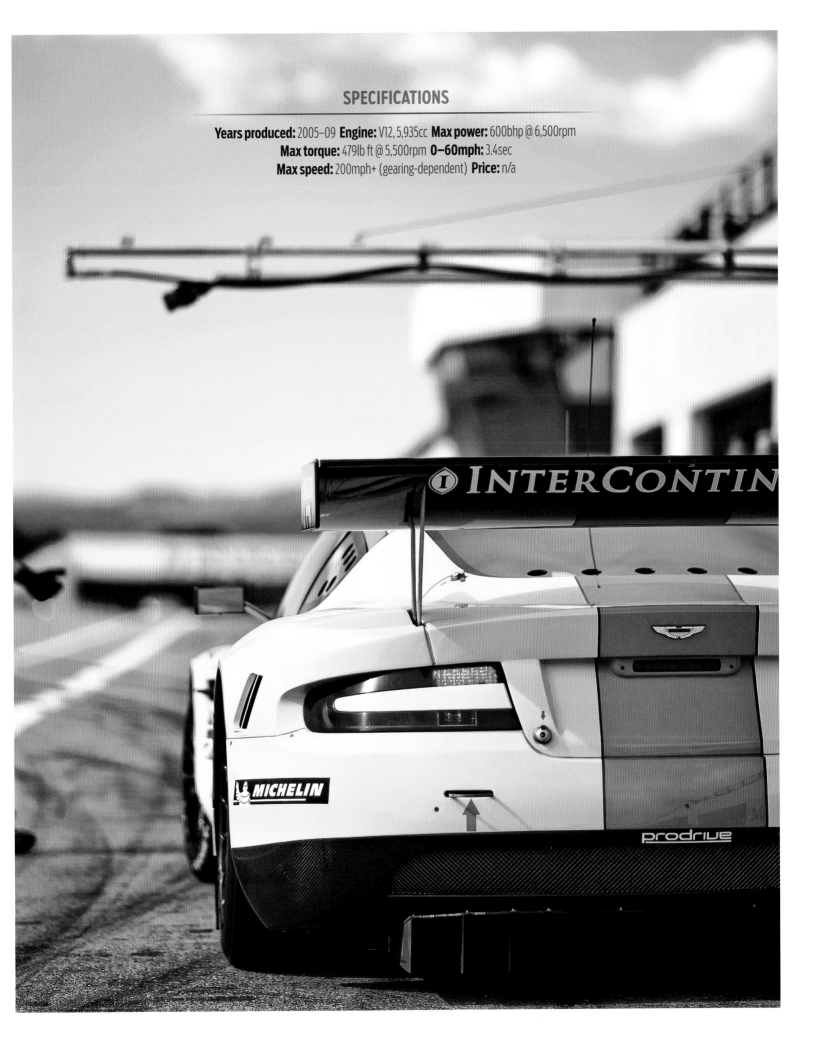

SPECIFICATIONS

Years produced: 2005–09 **Engine:** V12, 5,935cc **Max power:** 600bhp @ 6,500rpm
Max torque: 479lb ft @ 5,500rpm **0–60mph:** 3.4sec
Max speed: 200mph+ (gearing-dependent) **Price:** n/a

DBR9

2005
V8 Vantage

Following hot on the heels of the DB9 came Aston Martin's new baby, the V8 Vantage.

It would go on to become the best-selling Aston yet

D esigned around the same basic structure as the DB9 that had arrived the previous year, the modern-era V8 Vantage made a similarly profound impression on press and public alike when it was launched in 2005. Aimed squarely at Porsche's 911, this was an Aston that revelled in a more energetic brief. It delivered, too, shifting perceptions away from the grandiose, big-boned GTs of the 1990s and appealing to a more youthful catchment of enthusiasts for whom the Astons of yore were well out of reach financially and out of touch dynamically.

A strict two-seater, the V8 Vantage is an unapologetic sports car. Minimal overhangs and a muscled physique ensure it occupies a modest amount of road, while the stiff, light, aluminium structure and front-mid-engined layout promise agility of an altogether different magnitude to any previous Aston. The interior combines almost architectural design themes and modern, contrasting finishes and materials to create a sharp, contemporary ambience.

The driving position is low, the dashboard high, so you really feel like you're wearing the car rather than merely being perched in it. Early V8s were manual-only (an optional Sportshift automated sequential manual gearbox came in

2007), which suited the purist ethos of the Vantage perfectly. The gear lever is mounted too far back in the transmission tunnel for total ease, but the shift itself is quick enough.

The Jaguar-derived 4.3-litre V8, which made its debut in the Vantage, is a rowdy motor. It growls exuberantly and bellows when you work it hard. And you will be, it needs revs to deliver the promise of 380bhp and 302lb ft of torque. That's no chore, but it does mean you need to be tuned-in to the car, and be prepared to stir that six-speed manual gearbox to get the best from it (the 420bhp 4.7-litre version, which arrived in 2008, had considerably more punch).

Fortunately, the rest of the car is well up for the fight, thanks to tight damping, strong brakes, near-perfect 49:51 weight distribution, quick, informative and super-accurate steering and a brilliant balance of grip to grunt. This is a car you can – and will want to – drive to its limits, on road and perhaps on track, too (Aston's engineers spent months honing the V8 Vantage on the Nürburgring Nordschleife).

Compared with the DB9, it's a little less supple and trades refinement for a steelier edge, but if you're after a truly sporting coupé that will attack a country road like no Aston before it, there's little to touch the V8 Vantage.

SPECIFICATIONS

Years produced: 2005–17 **Engine:** V8, 4,281cc (4.3) **Max power:** 380bhp @ 7,000rpm
Max torque: 302lb ft @ 5,000rpm **0–60mph:** 4.8sec **Max speed:** 175mph
Price: £79,995/$110,000 new in 2005, £30,000+/$58,500+ today

SPECIFICATIONS

Years produced: 2007–12 **Engine:** V12, 5,935cc **Max power:** 510bhp @ 6,500rpm
Max torque: 420lb ft @ 5,750rpm **0–60mph:** 4.2sec **Max speed:** 191mph
Price: £160,000/$260,000 new in 2007, £80,000+/$166,900 today

2007
DBS

Replacing the Vanquish as Aston Martin's new flagship, the DBS was dismissed by some as a DB9 in a body kit. Big mistake

Ah, the Bond effect. There's no question the DBS was a highly desirable machine in its own right, but its coolness went up a few extra notches when it was revealed as the latest MI6 pool car for a certain 00 agent in 2006's brilliant *Casino Royale*. That was just as well, because initial press reaction to the DBS was somewhat lukewarm.

With a name resurrected from the early 1970s, the DBS took over from the V12 Vanquish as Aston Martin's flagship model but, put bluntly, some doubted it had the credentials. Rather than being a completely new, stand-alone model, as the Vanquish had been, the new car was clearly derived from the DB9, though its deep, sculpted chin, heavily vented bonnet and DBR9-inspired sills and rear diffuser transformed it into an altogether more potent-looking machine.

The V12 engine was similarly pumped-up, peak power rising from 450bhp to a far more serious-sounding 510bhp. Mated to a six-speed manual gearbox, it dropped the 0–60mph time to 4.2 seconds and lifted the top speed to over 190mph. Suspension and brakes were beefed-up to match, with ceramic discs among the new hardware. While not quite into outright supercar territory, this was one hardcore super-GT.

It was far more involving than the DB9, though not always for the right reasons. Early cars showed a distinct lack of composure in the chassis department, but later examples are much better tied-down. You really have to be on your mettle to drive the DBS to its full potential, but it really rewards when you do. On twisting back roads it feels lithe, 'threadable' and immensely quick, with accurate, well-weighted steering and exemplary body control. Just watch that tail. You can easily find yourself deploying some rapid 'opposite-lockery', even with traction control engaged. It's a reminder that, thing of sonic beauty that the mighty V12 is, it packs a brutal punch.

In late 2008, Aston introduced a Touchtronic option using the ZF six-speed auto with paddleshifts from the DB9 and a tougher casing for the transmission, beefier internals and a new management system. It worked well, while pressing Sport gave full manual control, with beautifully judged rev-matching on the way down the gears. The auto option widened the DBS's appeal, and maybe softened it, too. But the core character remained intact. With its extra power, harder-edged dynamics and ever-so-slightly dangerous demeanour, the DBS would always be Mr Hyde to the DB9's Dr Jekyll.

SPECIFICATIONS

Years produced: 2009–13 **Engine:** V12, 5,935cc **Max power:** 510bhp @ 6,500rpm
Max torque: 420lb ft @ 5,750rpm **0–60mph:** 4.1sec **Max speed:** 190mph
Price: £135,000/$180,000 new in 2009, £75,000+/$98,500+ today

2009
V12 Vantage

It was a deliciously mad concept – squeezing the biggest engine into the most compact car –
and it created one of the greatest Astons of recent times

I t was on **11 December 2007**, at a launch party for its new design studio at Gaydon, that Aston Martin chose to unveil a rather special project on which its top engineers had been quietly beavering away. They called it the V12 Vantage RS Concept. The official line was that it might make limited production, if there was sufficient interest…

A little over a year later, the V12 Vantage (no longer RS) emerged in production form, powered by the 510bhp V12 from the DBS. The RS's active rear aerofoil had been dropped, but otherwise it was remarkably true to the concept, right down to the bonnet vents, essential to keep the V12 cool.

The extra weight of the engine (around 100kg/220lb) was offset by extensive use of carbon fibre (in the bonnet, diffuser, seats and brakes) so the eventual overall weight penalty was just 50kg (110lb). The result was virtually supercar levels of performance. Aston Martin claimed a top speed of 190mph and 0–60mph in 4.1 seconds, and although independent road-testers couldn't quite match that (*evo* recorded 4.4 seconds, with 0–100mph in 9.7), the V12V was widely acclaimed as the most exciting Aston in pure driving terms for many a long year.

Early cars all came with a good old-fashioned stick-shift gearbox, a Graziano six-speeder. There was a mechanical limited-slip differential, along with three-stage electronic traction control. The braking system featured the DBS's massive carbon-ceramic discs, the conventional fixed-rate dampers were tuned to give a firm ride, and the tyres were near-track-spec Pirelli P Zero Corsas. These offered phenomenal grip on warm, dry roads – and scarily little purchase on cold, wet ones.

In the dry, on a give-and-take-road where you're constantly slowing and accelerating, the V12 is brutal. Whatever gear, whatever revs, the shrink-wrapped engine leaps forward as soon as your right foot flexes. No lag, no wind-up, it's as though you've instantly hit the supercar sweet spot every time you accelerate. Grip is phenomenal, the whole car much more connected to the surface of the road than either a V8 Vantage or DBS, and the alacrity of direction changes just what you'd expect from such a short wheelbase. But then you're sitting in a fixed-back carbon bucket seat and holding an Alcantara-covered steering wheel for a reason: the V12 Vantage is no freakish, over-engineered dragster, no soft straight-line train – it is a gentleman's road-racer.

2009
One-77

Aston Martin's engineers were given free rein to produce the ultimate analogue supercar.

The stupendous One-77 was the result

SPECIFICATIONS

Years produced: 2009–12 **Engine:** V12, 7,312cc **Max power:** 750bhp @ 7,600rpm
Max torque: 553lb ft @ 5,000rpm **0–60mph:** 3.6sec **Max speed:** 220mph+
Price: £1.15million/$1.8 million new, £1.75 million+/$2.18 million+ today

L ow and wide, but pinched tight at the waist to give the shape almost indecent curves, the One-77 is sculpted with a razor-sharp tension. In the middle of nowhere with only sheep and beautiful roads for company, deep in a city centre or rolling under the sodium lights of a motorway… the One-77 would look jaw-dropping wherever you put it. Especially if somebody opened the door and told you the car was all yours, for today at least.

If the startling looks and the ferocious impatience of the V12 even at idle hadn't already given it away, the thick carbon-fibre sill is the final telltale that this is a very different sort of Aston Martin. That carbon-fibre monocoque is, of course, incredibly light (180kg/397lb) and stiff, the thrillingly modern structure clothed with handcrafted aluminium panels. It's still an Aston Martin, after all.

Another nod to tradition is the front engine/rear-wheel-drive configuration, although in this instance the radically revised Cosworth-developed 7.3-litre V12 is mounted well behind the front axle and 100mm (4in) lower in the chassis than in a DB9 or Vanquish. The engine itself is dry-sumped, the compression ratio up to 10.9:1, and it produces a head-spinning 750bhp at 7,600rpm and 553lb ft at 5,000rpm. It

drives through a six-speed transaxle-operated gearbox via paddles mounted on the steering column. Should you find the room, a derestricted road and a bottle full of brave pills, the One-77 can reach over 220mph.

The driver's door zips open almost weightlessly and you drop carefully down into the exquisite interior. It's an oddly calm experience, the thick carbon fibre muting the outside world so you get that heavy, gloopy silence as you might on a snowy day, and all around is cool leather and expensively polished weave.

Aim the heavy chunk of crystal at the spring-loaded slot in the middle of the starter button and press it until it's swallowed. The V12 spits furiously through the quad-exit exhausts hidden in the rear diffuser. Eeek. Now just click the right-hand paddle to select first and take a deep breath.

The calmness disappears as soon as that V12 shatters the silence, and as the automated clutch clumsily disengages and the One-77 judders and jerks away with all the grace of a rhino on ice skates, it's replaced by almost blind panic. Road-noise hums back through the chassis – a common trait with cars constructed of this exotic material – and the V12's sharp howl seems to swirl around you like a raging thunderstorm.

The gearbox isn't happy at low speeds and the changes *thunk* home almost reluctantly, the ride is very firm and the instantaneous throttle response and sheer volume of the V12 all add up to a pretty intimidating experience. Cover a few more miles, however, and you start to revel in the accuracy of the steering response, the stability of the chassis when you change direction with little or no sense of inertia, and the

guiding hand of the traction and stability systems. Press the Sport button on the sweeping centre console and you get full access to the torque, while the noise – improbably – ratchets up still further.

The fact is, the One-77 is a totally different animal from any other modern Aston Martin. The stiffness of the chassis, the low centre of gravity and the motorsport-derived, inboard, fully adjustable suspension create a much more agile platform and there's such clarity to the controls. Although the flat-sided steering wheel looks odd, it feels just right, and the rack's speed and relatively light weighting are a perfect match to a chassis that feels wide-tracked and eager to change direction.

DSC Track Mode gives a little more leeway before stepping in to tidy up the driver's mess. In fact it's well judged and allows you to delve deeper, to drive through the little trace of understeer and feel the rear tyres start to neutralize the balance and then slip into a sliver of oversteer. That said, if you're clumsy with the throttle, it can start to tie itself in knots, holding you back through the middle of the corner but then setting the rear tyres free just as you straighten out with a wicked, heart-attack-inducing spike of wheelspin.

No question, the One-77 can feel hellishly scary and you have to be wary of the engine's sharpness at the top end of the rev-range. So it demands real concentration to drive quickly. For some it will be too hardcore, and certainly the relaxing GT qualities of the DB9 or the contemporary Vanquish have been sacrificed for more response and agility. But then the One-77 delivers a unique, intense and focused driving experience that's a match for any supercar you'd care to mention.

2010
Rapide

An Aston for the family man, the Rapide is a surprisingly rare and seriously under-appreciated machine

SPECIFICATIONS

Years produced: 2010–12 **Engine:** V12, 5,935cc **Max power:** 470bhp @ 6,000rpm
Max torque: 443lb ft @ 5,000rpm **0–60mph:** 5.2sec **Max speed:** 188mph
Price: £139,950/$197,850 new in 2010, £65,000+/$89,600+ today

When Porsche revealed it was launching a four-seat, five-door saloon, it didn't take long for Aston to respond. The Panamera appeared in April 2009; less than a year later, the first Rapides were rolling out of a dedicated facility at the Magna Steyr factory in Austria.

Boss Ulrich Bez outsourced production because he envisaged annual sales of 2,000 cars – far too many for Gaydon to cope with. In fact the Rapide never approached those numbers, and in 2012 production relocated to the UK. Indeed, the Rapide is one of the rarest of modern Astons.

At launch, the Rapide came with a 470bhp version of the familiar 5.9-litre V12, driving through a six-speed automatic transaxle gearbox with the option to shift manually via paddles – Touchtronic 2, in Aston-speak. The performance claims were 0–60 in 5.2 seconds and a top speed of 188mph. So it was rapid, and it looked great, so why were sales slow?

Some were no doubt deterred by its relatively cramped rear seats and limited luggage space; others, perhaps, by the wilfully sporting character of its chassis and drivetrain. Aston always described it as a four-seater sports car, and it

wasn't kidding. Despite its extra length (250mm/10in was added to the wheelbase) and weight, the Rapide is every bit as agile and involving as a DB9, with which it shared most of its underpinnings.

You're aware that there's more mass along for the ride, but, that said, the button to select a firmer damper setting goes un-pushed because the big Aston is quite firmly sprung, nicely taut and feels rewardingly precise as it is. What's more, the ideally weighted steering feels more natural than in other Astons of the period. It has a faster rack rate than the DB9 in order to give it the same feeling of agility – and it does that and more. There's an easy, natural feel to its dynamics and, when you ask, it delivers. The bottom line is that it's a more impressive steer than the DB9 or DBS.

Grip from the bespoke Bridgestone Potenza S001s is strong and there's hardly a flicker from the stability control light as the 470bhp V12 digs deep. That magnificent engine really comes alive from 3,000rpm, as if a dozen trumpet mutes are doffed in unison, the sound becoming heavy, gravelly, glorious. Surprising car, the Rapide…

2011

V12 Zagato

Based on the brilliant and dazzlingly quick V12 Vantage,

this Zagato Aston was as capable as it was collectable

SPECIFICATIONS

Years produced: 2011–12 **Engine:** V12, 5,935cc **Max power:** 510bhp @ 6,500rpm
Max torque: 420lb ft @ 5,750rpm **0–60mph:** 4.2sec **Max speed:** 190mph
Price: £396,000/$510,000 new in 2012, £350,000+/$435,450+ today

Though clearly wearing its Zagato signatures on its sleeve, the latest 'collaboration' was, in fact, designed by Aston Martin's own Marek Reichman. It didn't seem to matter – it couldn't be mistaken for anything other than an Aston Zagato, and the run of 101 cars was snapped up by wealthy aficionados. Those who took the trouble to drive it, rather than salt it away, discovered a car every bit as fine in its own way as the DB4 GT and V8 Zagatos of previous eras. The Vantage-based V12 Zagato looks incredibly compact and purposeful as you walk up to it, and you can't help spending a minute or two just drinking in all the details – things like the subtle curves of the roof and the carbon fibre-clad scoops in which the rear lights are set.

Inside feels a whole lot more dramatic than the regular Vantage, thanks to the bold, wavy stitching running through the leather. The sight of a gearstick protruding from the transmission tunnel is another source of joy, for it signifies this Zagato as one of the last great V12-engined cars to feature a manual gearbox. A product of 2011 it might be, but in many respects the V12 Zagato is an old soul and all the better for it. The 5.9-litre V12 punches into life with an exuberant flare of revs before settling into a relaxed idle, tailpipes humming to a mellow, muscular beat. All the major controls – steering, clutch and gearshift – have a satisfying, homogeneous weight

that suits the car. The ride is firm – not uncompromisingly so, but there's definitely an edge to it that suggests a no-nonsense character, with sharper responses than the regular V12 Vantage.

You don't need to work the V12 hard to sense its potential. Indeed, you can surf along on the low-rev torque, short-shifting through the six-speed gearbox and enjoying the elastic performance in the higher gears. Dig deeper and the urgency you unleash is almost startling, the V12 Zagato shifting from mild-mannered to malevolent as the tacho winds past 5,000rpm. The sound is sensational: a big-hearted fanfare that's animalistic in its rawness but symphonic in a way that only 12-cylinder engines can be.

Where an earlier car like the DB4 GT Zagato is about handling over grip, the V12 is much more about roadholding, as is the modern way. With over 500bhp, it has to be. The poise, body control, traction and, especially, the braking (via huge carbon-ceramic discs) are all light years ahead, as is the pace at which you can cover the ground. However, as with the DB4, it thrives on commitment, so if you're prepared to give your all, you'll find a car that needs skill and confidence to master yet works with you – indeed, relies upon you – to get the absolute best from it. An Aston Martin Zagato remains much more than just a pretty face.

V12 Zagato

2012
V12 Vantage Roadster

It was only a matter of time before Aston created a convertible version of its baby supercar.

The only surprise was that it built just 101 examples

T he soft option? If convertibles are supposed to be the slightly laid-back, less intense versions of their roofed siblings, no one told the team who created the V12V Roadster. In fact neither 'roadster' nor 'convertible' really does it justice. This is a sports car, red in tooth and claw.

As with the roadster version of the V8 Vantage, the V12V's structure was beefed up to compensate for the loss of the roof, with a stronger crossbeam behind the dash and thicker, more rigidly fixed aluminium undertrays to further boost structural strength. Unique to the V12 Roadster were a new rear damper and spring design.

As with the V12 coupé, it's what the aluminium chassis cradles that's really compelling, though: almost 6 litres, 48 valves, 510bhp and 420lb ft, hooked up to a six-speed manual gearbox. That's one heck of a setup for a car considerably shorter and lower than a 991-generation Porsche 911. And although the torque figures might suggest that the big motor needs some revs to get going, the truth is that it always feels beautifully and effortlessly muscular, despite the fact it's pushing a substantial 1,760kg (1.94 tons), some 80kg (176lb) more than the coupé version. That extra weight adds a couple of tenths to the 0–60 time; the claimed top speed is an identical 190mph.

The P Zero Corsas provide loads of traction. You have to manage a bit of turn-in understeer (but much less than expected with that big engine out front), maybe rolling in a little oversteer correction on corner exit. But the balance is very impressive, and in the dry you'll quickly be happy to disable the DSC (Dynamic Stability Control) altogether, although in the wet the Vantage feels a bit more spiky. You'd keep learning more about this car every day for a very long time.

Top down, you're free to revel in the full, widescreen, surround-sound experience. There's just enough fresh air swirling around the top of your head to get the sense of exposure, but because you're sat low in the car you also have that delicious feeling of warmth and security. And the noise. Oh the noise! All-pervading, all-encompassing, it percolates to your very soul, a rousing, brassy bellow on full power, punctuated by percussive pops and crackles as you back off and blip-blip-blip down the gears. You always feel connected to the V12V Roadster, but with the roof down you get that final ten per cent of sensory engagement that elevates the experience beyond even the V12 Vantage coupé. Why Aston Martin limited the production run to just 101 remains a mystery, but the owners of those cars aren't complaining!

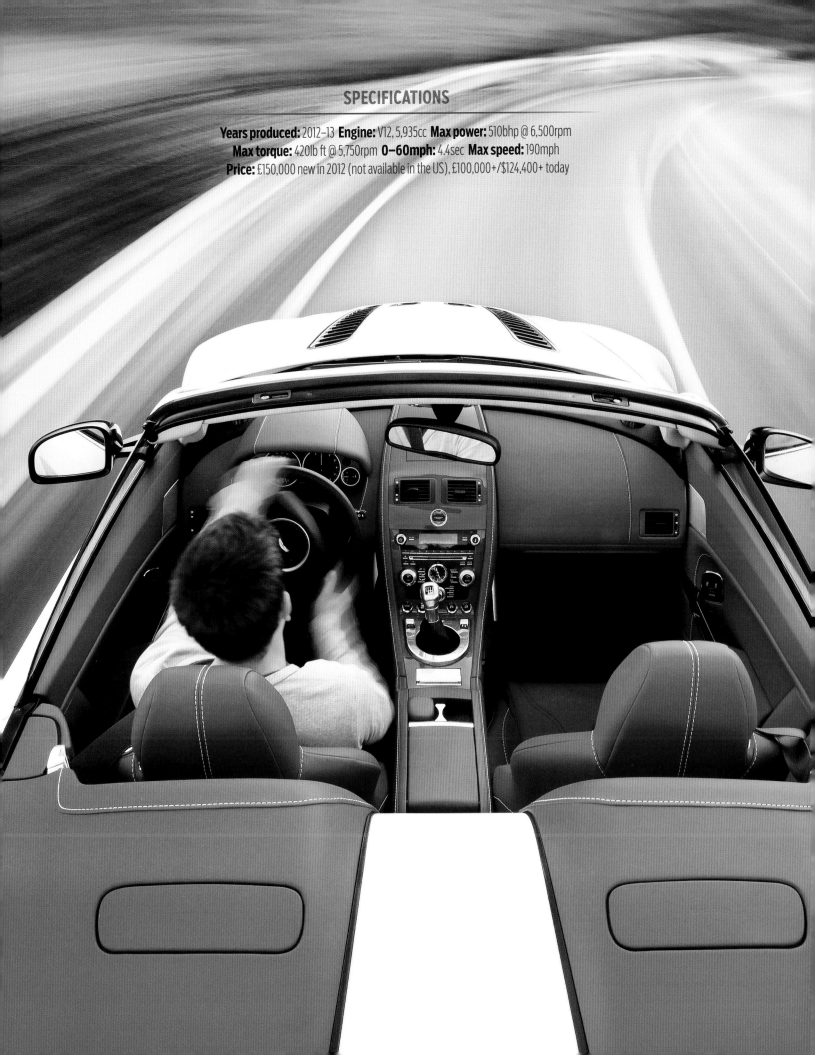

SPECIFICATIONS

Years produced: 2012–13 **Engine:** V12, 5,935cc **Max power:** 510bhp @ 6,500rpm
Max torque: 420lb ft @ 5,750rpm **0–60mph:** 4.4sec **Max speed:** 190mph
Price: £150,000 new in 2012 (not available in the US), £100,000+/$124,400+ today

2012

Vanquish

Replacing the DBS as Aston Martin's mainstream production flagship, the new Vanquish had a lot

to live up to – including the Vanquish name

SPECIFICATIONS

Years produced: 2012–17 **Engine:** V12, 5,935cc **Max power:** 565bhp @ 6,750rpm
Max torque: 457lb ft @ 5,500rpm **0–60mph:** 4.0sec **Max speed:** 183mph (six-speed)
Price: £190,000/$280,000 new in 2012, £120,000+/$172,800+ today

D usting off the Vanquish badge in 2012 for a new range-topper was a bold statement. The original had been a landmark car, and one of the most revered Astons of recent times. Could the new Vanquish make a similar impact and re-establish Aston as a maker of world-class super-GTs?

The key facts suggested it could. The new car had full carbon-fibre bodywork, the latest generation of the VH aluminium structure providing a 25 per cent stiffer platform, a reworked V12 mounted 13mm (½in) lower and producing a storming 565bhp, and a 0–60mph time of 4 seconds dead. It looked every inch the super-GT, too, incorporating design elements from the One-77 supercar, its lean, sculptural forms clearly distancing itself from the brutal DBS.

But the acid test, as ever, is on the road and here, too, the Vanquish is a clear step on from the DBS. The updated model that arrived in 2014 would benefit from the introduction of a new, eight-speed gearbox, but even an early car with the six-speed paddleshift Touchtronic 2 auto is an event – especially on a mountain road that's every bit as dramatic as the Vanquish's performance.

As the road climbs, Touchtronic 2 is in manual mode, while a little red light on the Sport button of the beautifully sculpted steering wheel signals that the exhaust is in naughty

mode, the steering weight is beefed up and throttle response is at its sharpest.

The ADS (Adaptive Damping System) is in Sport mode, too. The dampers, suspended by double wishbones all-round, are continuously variable, but the Normal, Sport and Track modes dictate the parameters within which they work. On a road that seems to be struggling to stop the earth below from bursting through, you leave the Track setting for another day. So the car is optimized for the here and now. And you know what? It feels different. In a good way.

It's thanks to that new, lighter, stiffer chassis, which permeates every control. The steering is smoother and rarely gets that nasty corrugated judder that affects earlier VH-platform Astons. You just know it's located better and that it's turning wheels that are in tune with the surface. The ride is quite hard in Sport but the damping only ever needs one bite to deal with bumps, and the turn-in response and mid-corner feel is so much more secure thanks to that efficiency.

The Vanquish also has superb traction in the dry and feels less edgy than the sometimes unpredictable DBS. Skimming over crests, plunging into left-right compressions and thumping out of tight hairpins, it's hooked-up and agile.

The V12 engine has always liked revs and now it really has an appetite above 5,500rpm, the point where the DBS started to feel a bit strangled.

The only mild disappointment with an early example is the Touchtronic 2 transmission – a six-speed ZF torque-converter automatic with paddleshift. Around town it's refined and slips into the background, but it lacks the creamy seamlessness of the new-generation ZF eight-speed automatic (which, of course, would arrive in 2014).

The chassis is the big news, though. There's no sudden breakaway unless you really provoke it. And while that kind of stability might sound a little dull for some, the reality is that it makes the Vanquish wonderfully exploitable and allows you to drive the car very close to its limits, scratching out every last bit of grip, using the carbon-ceramic brakes to their full potential.

Of course, you can still turn off the DSC (Dynamic Stability Control) altogether, and there's little to fear from doing so. The electronics have clearly been optimized to work with an already well-sorted chassis rather than tame any nasty handling characteristics, so the Vanquish's neutral and progressive balance remains intact.

The VH chassis architecture has moved on markedly, and you can sense the added rigidity of the platform and the clean responses that it allows. In terms of damping, balance, agility and progressiveness, the Vanquish is ostensibly a new car and a much better one than the DBS. While not a landmark like the original Vanquish, it's still a fine super-GT.

Vanquish

2013
Rapide S

The slow-selling Rapide was given a thorough refresh in 2013, including a bold new face.
It still wants to be a sports car...

The Rapide never sold in the numbers that Aston Martin envisaged and, in January 2013, the original car was replaced by the Rapide S. A deeper grille and new headlight treatment ramped up the road presence, but this was more than a facelift. Under the bonnet, variable valve timing and a new management system for the latest version of the V12 engine lifted peak power from 470 to 550bhp, dropping the 0–60mph time to just 4.9 seconds and raising the top speed to 190mph.

Ever since its launch, the Rapide has been lauded for its beauty, quality and dynamism, but criticized for its derivative looks, awkward rear access and a lack of rear occupant space. While there's no question the more aggressive grille and headlight treatment have given it a stronger identity, and the new 550bhp 'Gen4' quad cam V12 engine has sharpened its performance still further, even such an extensive revamp can't address those perceived shortcomings. It may have four seats but the Rapide S is very definitely a sports car first, luxury car second. And more than ever a delight to drive.

The adaptive damping gives you increasingly firm settings, while a Sport mode sharpens the throttle response and gearshift times of the six-speed paddleshift automatic and opens the throats of the twin exhausts to emit a deliciously raucous bellow.

From the moment you turn the steering wheel or caress the throttle, the Rapide S seduces you with its abundant urge and smoothly measured control. The steering is weighty and connected, the engine hugely muscular, the ride firm but rounded in a way many 190mph cars fail to manage. When you have the opportunity, it really does fire you down the road like a true sports car, with grip levels, traction and braking to match.

It also loves long distances, but it's always egging you on to take the twisty way to your destination. Whatever the journey, there's no question it's a beguiling car and one that's an event to drive or be driven in.

In late 2014, the S was given an extensive refresh, which included the latest, brilliant eight-speed Touchtronic 3 gearbox, along with tauter suspension and a host of detail refinements. The revised gearing and a small increase in power enabled Aston Martin to claim a truly astonishing 203mph and 0–60 in a faintly ridiculous 4.2 seconds. More than ever, the Rapide was Aston's four-seater sports car.

SPECIFICATIONS

Years produced: 2013- **Engine:** V12, 5,935cc **Max power:** 550bhp @ 6,000rpm
Max torque: 457lb ft @ 5,000rpm **0–60mph:** 4.9sec **Max speed:** 190mph
Price: £149,995/$198,250 new in 2013, £80,000+/$127,800 today

2013

V12 Vantage S

Even more power, and now a 200mph+ top speed... Aston's pocket rocket was back,
even more gloriously bonkers than ever

SPECIFICATIONS

Years produced: 2013–17 **Engine:** V12, 5,935cc **Max power:** 565bhp @ 6,750rpm
Max torque: 457lb ft @ 5,750rpm **0–60mph:** 3.7sec **Max speed:** 205mph
Price: £138,000/$185,000 new in 2013, £90,000+/$125,800+ today

Aston Martin had announced that V12 Vantage production would end in June 2013, but any tinge of disappointment was chased away by the announcement of its replacement, the V12 Vantage S. With a new Bosch engine management system and variable camshaft timing, Aston's engineers had extracted a further 55bhp from the V12, lifting peak output to 565bhp. This was the same engine that had appeared in the new Vanquish; installed in the smaller, lighter Vantage, the results were sensational.

Mated for the first time to the seven-speed Sportshift paddle-operated gearbox (the stick shift was now officially dead), it gave genuine supercar performance: the 0–60mph time was slashed to 3.7 seconds and top speed was a claimed 205mph. It was the quickest series-production Aston to date; only the One-77 hypercar was faster.

A year later, in summer 2014, the 201mph V12 Vantage S Roadster joined the range, becoming the fastest Aston convertible to date. And then, for fans of the traditional gear lever, in autumn 2016 the V12 V S was made available with a seven-speed manual gearbox…

The manual gearbox is a seven-speed unit derived from the paddleshift gearbox. Aston hasn't held back on the nostalgia, placing first gear in the classic dogleg position (far left and back from neutral) with the remaining six forward gears arranged in a conventional H-pattern. It does mean you have to give yourself time to learn your way around the gearbox, but then that powerhouse of a V12 will pull pretty much any gear at any revs.

The engineers also developed AMSHIFT, which is basically a cheat for those who never mastered heel-and-toe throttle-blip downshifts. Engaged by pressing and holding the Sport button, the automated whoop-whoops are great fun!

But it's the performance that stays with you. There's always been something wondrous about the concept of a car as compact as the Vantage concealing a stonking V12, and the V12VS takes this to a new level. The sense of explosive power makes your heart pump every time you touch the throttle; the knowledge that tyres and torque are constantly warring factions is enough to make your mouth go dry. No series-production Aston has ever felt more ferocious than this car.

SPECIFICATIONS

Years produced: 2013 **Engine:** V12, 5,935cc **Max power:** 565bhp @ 6,750rpm
Max torque: 457lb ft @ 5,750rpm **0–60mph:** 4.0sec
Max speed: 180mph **Price:** n/a

2013
CC100

Built to celebrate Aston Martin's 100th birthday, the CC100 was to be a one-off,

until a wealthy customer persuaded Aston to build a second

T he initial idea was simple enough: to create an ultra-special, one-off model to celebrate Aston Martin's centenary year in 2013. Senior designer Miles Nurnberger and design boss Marek Reichman decided on a modern take on a 1950s endurance racer – with obvious nods to Aston's 1959 Le Mans-winning DBR1.

While the result may look like a motor-show special, the CC100 was designed and built not just to be driven but to be used. So it shared its underpinnings with the V12 Vantage Roadster, the inherent flexibility of Aston's VH chassis architecture making it a relatively simple process to design new bodywork to fit over the same hardpoints.

That bodywork is made entirely from carbon fibre, with 55 separate mouldings. A distinctive feature is the opening safety bars: narrow vestigial doors with a 'gull' opening. They allow the car to keep the side aperture that was part of the design brief from the start – one of the car's defining features was to be the sensation of air rushing past. And a top spotter's detail: the shape of each side opening is half of the Aston Martin winged badge. The wheelbase and the basic chassis are identical to those of the Vantage, and the

electrical architecture, stability control system and brakes are also identical, for simplicity's sake. The CC100 has a wider body, necessitating a 100mm (4in) increase in track, achieved through new control arms at the front and a widened subframe and longer drive shafts at the rear. The suspension features standard springs and four-way adjustable dampers.

The engine is the 565bhp version of the 5.9-litre V12, as seen in the new Vanquish and V12 Vantage S, mated to a single-clutch automated transmission with paddleshifts. With a 1,370-kg (1.5-ton) kerb weight representing a substantial saving over the standard V12 Vantage Roadster's 1,760kg (1.94 tons), performance was guaranteed to be electrifying.

Throughout 2013, the CC100 could be seen in action at various Aston centenary events, including a parade lap of the Nürburgring, and then it was off to its new owner who, according to Aston, planned to drive it regularly. It was later revealed that a second car would be built for another ultra-wealthy buyer. Although there was no official price, the rumour was that each CC100 would be costing its new owner a 'mid-ranking six-figure sum'. Now that is one expensive birthday present.

2013
DB9

Relaunched in 2013, the new – and much-improved –

DB9 was as gorgeous as ever, but with a little added edge

SPECIFICATIONS

Years produced: 2013–16 **Engine:** V12, 5,935cc **Max power:** 510bhp @ 6,500rpm
Max torque: 457lb ft @ 5,500rpm **0–60mph:** 4.5sec **Max speed:** 183mph
Price: £131,995/$183,700 new in 2013, £80,000+/$114,600 today

Anyone remember the Virage? Not the early-1990s, Gauntlett-era bruiser, but the 2011 DB9-based model that was shoehorned into the model line-up between the DB9 and the DBS? The idea was to create a more aggressive car than the DB9 that wasn't as extreme as the DBS. So it had more power and a subtle restyle that included a deeper front splitter and a slightly more aggressive sill treatment. It was a niche too far and after about a year the Virage was quietly dropped. But the restyle lived on in the thoroughly updated DB9, for the 2013 model year.

The changes for this second-gen DB9 were far more than skin-deep. The V12 benefited from lessons learned in the Vanquish programme. Tuned for a more relaxed, 'torquey' delivery peak power is still up from 469bhp to 510bhp, with 457lb ft available at 5,500rpm. The new DB9 shaves a couple of tenths off its former 0–60mph sprint at 4.5 seconds and tops out at 183mph. The VH aluminium architecture is 20 per cent stiffer, and the V12 engine itself sits lower in the chassis. Ostensibly to improve pedestrian safety, this has the additional benefit of lowering the centre of gravity. Carbon-ceramic brakes are now standard on the DB9, saving around

12.5kg (27½lb) in unsprung weight as well as improving braking performance and resistance to fade, and the ADS (Adaptive Damping System) has been retuned. It's a thorough and comprehensive update.

This DB9 veers more to the control of a sports car than the soothing attributes of a GT. The ride, even with the ADS in Normal, is pretty firm, and the aluminium chassis transmits more road noise than you might expect. Any disappointment is tempered by the sheer sense of connection that the DB9 offers, though. The steering really is superb, isolating larger lumps and bumps but allowing the surface's texture to bubble back to the wheel. Brake-feel is another standout feature, and DSC (Dynamic Stability Control) track mode is utterly brilliant – allowing you to really lean on the front tyres and then load the rears with all that power but acting like a magical talent-enhancer to keep you out of the undergrowth.

Best DB9? Unquestionably. It's dazzlingly quick when you use the full rev range, the chassis is better balanced than ever, and the stiffer chassis and weight savings create a car overflowing with feedback. These final DB9s, including the run-out GT model, would be a tough act to follow.

Vantage GT12

One hundred kilos (220lb) lighter than a regular V12 Vantage S and with even more power, the track-inspired GT12 is about as extreme as a road car gets

Wild wings and warpaint – not, it must be said, things ordinarily associated with Aston Martin road cars. But then there's nothing remotely ordinary about the Vantage GT12. A special-series model built in a strictly limited run of 100 cars and costing £250,000/$311,500 before any options, it's an emphatic last hurrah for the current Vantage range.

With 592bhp (up 27bhp on the 'regular' V12 Vantage S) and weighing a substantial 100kg (220lb) less, it's easily the most potent Vantage of the modern era. And that potency is underpinned by wide-track suspension, aerodynamic downforce and giant carbon-ceramic brakes, while the multi-mode damping, stability and ABS systems have all been recalibrated to match its greater performance.

As with the exterior, which is formed largely from lightweight carbon fibre, the interior is a cocoon of carefully crafted composites, the ambience tilted in favour of motorsport-infused minimalism, though satnav, air-con and the optional Bang & Olufsen hi-fi ensure you still have some creature comforts.

Given those looks, you might expect the GT12 to be a prickly and short-tempered road car, but, far from sacrificing on-road manners, it's remarkably well behaved. The seven-speed Sportshift III gearbox (there's no manual option) means it's a cinch to simply jump in and drive. The steering feels a little lighter and freer, with brighter and more detailed feedback. Its rate of response is perfectly judged to give genuine agility, but not so much that it destabilizes the rear end, so there's perfect unison in the way it changes direction.

Better still, the electronic stability control allows the car to work beneath you – just enough to require small steering corrections – but when you need help, it gives it, intervening smoothly and calmly like an unseen hand. The carbon-ceramic brakes are simply tireless.

The enhanced V12 is undoubtedly one of the most sensational internal combustion engines money can buy. There's tons of torque, so you don't need to dig too deep for the GT12 to feel mighty, but its appetite for revs is such that the deeper you do dig, the more you find. For the fortunate 100, the GT12 is sure to be a highlight of their collections.

SPECIFICATIONS

Years produced: 2015–16 **Engine:** V12, 5,935cc **Max power:** 592bhp @ 7,000rpm
Max torque: 461lb ft @ 5,500rpm **0–60mph:** 3.5sec **Max speed:** 185mph
Price: £250,000 new (plus options, car not available in the US), c.£250,000/$311,050 today

Lagonda Taraf

The Lagonda badge hadn't been seen since the late 1980s, but in 2015 it was back –

and the inspiration for the new Taraf was obvious

SPECIFICATIONS

Years produced: 2015– **Engine:** V12, 5,935cc **Max power:** 540bhp @ 6,650rpm
Max torque: 465lb ft @ 5,500rpm **0–60mph:** 4.4sec
Max speed: 195mph+ **Price:** £696,000/c. $1,000,000 new

Back in the 1980s, the wedge-shaped Lagonda was a particular hit with Middle Eastern buyers, who accounted for about half of them. And that was exactly the market at which Aston Martin was pitching the Taraf when it relaunched the Lagonda marque.

The clue was in the name: 'Taraf' translates approximately as 'luxury' in Arabic, a moniker that tallies appropriately with the car's sky-high price. Only 200 would be built, although that was a doubling of the initial projected run, an increase made possible by making it EU-compliant. That, in turn, opened up sales into other global regions, and the Taraf would be available in left- or right-hand drive.

Styling-wise, too, the Taraf was inspired by the V8 wedge: both cars are long, lean and low. Underneath, the Taraf is basically a stretched Rapide S, but one that has been softened a touch to make it better suited to its limousine role. Power has been slightly reduced: 550bhp down to 540bhp. Thanks to the use of carbon fibre for the bodyshell's outer panels, the Taraf's weight was kept to almost exactly that of a Rapide S, at 2,000kg (2.2 tons). Performance, then, is hardly lacking, with a stated 0–60mph time of 4.4 seconds and top speed 'in excess of' 195mph.

The cabin is beautifully appointed and immaculately finished. Press home the now-familiar crystal key fob and the engine fires with a muted roar rather than with a strident bark. Select 'Drive' – the Taraf has the latest Touchtronic 3 eight-speed transmission – and waft away on a breath of throttle. While the car doesn't feel in the least bit unwieldy, you are always conscious of that extra 20cm (7¾in) in the wheelbase, especially when turning out of a junction or negotiating a tight roundabout. The whole car measures 5.4m (17¾ft) from tip to tail – 38cm (15in) longer than a Rapide S. The ride is moderately supple, tempered by the underlying tension that characterizes all modern performance cars.

But the Taraf is, one suspects, a trophy car, an object to collect, rather than a working tool. Let's not be too critical, therefore. Let's just be grateful that it exists.

Vulcan

The Vulcan started life as a track version of the One-77 supercar,

then morphed into something even more extreme

SPECIFICATIONS

Years produced: 2015–16 **Engine:** V12, 7,000cc **Max power:** 820bhp @ 7,750rpm
Max torque: 575lb ft @ 6,500rpm **0–60mph:** sub3.0sec
Max speed: 200mph+ **Price:** £1.8 million/$2.3 million new in 2015, £2 million+/$2.49 million+ today

The ultimate rich man's plaything, the Vulcan is what happens when Aston Martin's designers and engineers are given free rein to create the ultimate track-day car. Loosely based on One-77 underpinnings, the Vulcan has a 7-litre version of Aston's GT3-spec V12, mated to a racing sequential transmission. Add race-spec suspension, brakes and quite literally a ton of downforce and you have the most extreme Aston yet driven. With a run of just 24 cars, one of the rarest and most expensive, too.

You sit a long way back, the GT3-style steering wheel fitting snugly in your gloved hands. An innocent-looking rotary switch controls the Vulcan's power output. Each click takes you up a notch, from 550bhp shopping mode to 675 and, finally, the full-on 820. Then all that remains is to take a deep breath and fire the V12 into life.

The noise is one to make your mouth dry and your palms moisten. It's a fast, feral, mechanical sound – raw but refined, cultured but blessed with the instantaneous response of a competition car. Clamped into the seat by shoulder- and lap-straps, the car feels like an extension of your body. Push on the heavy clutch, pull back on the right-hand paddle and hear first gear engage with a solid ker-chunk and you're away.

The Vulcan responds immediately and precisely to every input, but while you might fear it would be nervous and impatient, it's approachable and tolerant. It encourages rather than goads you, so with every lap you feel happy to hold each gear for longer, squeeze more insistently on the throttle, charge deeper into the braking zones and lean harder on the invisible support of downforce. There's nothing to touch a big, rampant, naturally aspirated V12 for physicality and a sense of endless, screaming power. The mechanical and aerodynamic grip produced by those huge Michelin slicks and colossal aerokit is fearsome, but the Vulcan communicates its limits clearly and consistently, and the balance is nicely neutral.

The Vulcan delivers intense physical and emotional highs, an experience so far removed from mere mortal cars as to make you redefine what you thought was possible – and what you thought an Aston Martin could be.

Vulcan

SPECIFICATIONS

Years produced: 2016–17 **Engine:** V8, 4,753cc **Max power:** 440bhp @ 7,300rpm
Max torque: 361lb ft @ 5,000rpm **0–60mph:** 4.4sec
Max speed: 190mph **Price:** £165,000+ new (not available in the US)

2016
Vantage GT8

This track-inspired GT8 is the ultimate evolution of the current V8 Vantage.

Could it possibly be as wild as it looks?

Aston Martin is no stranger to the road-racer breed, going right back to the DB4 GT, and in recent years it has built a number of special-series cars inspired by its racing machines, including 2015's spectacular Vantage GT12. So with clear parallels between the eight-cylinder Vantage and the current Vantage GTE World Endurance Championship cars, it was a logical – and welcome – step to use the same recipe to create the GT8. One hundred and fifty of them, to be precise, with a starting price of £165,000. And all snapped up before the first car was delivered.

Clad in a battledress of carbon-fibre panels, sculpted and chiselled for maximum aerodynamic and aesthetic effect, the GT8 is the lightest and most powerful eight-cylinder Vantage ever, the product of a design and engineering team let off the leash. Power is up, but by just 10bhp, to a respectable 440bhp. However, weight is down by as much as 100kg (220lb) – to 1,510kg (1.66 tons) – depending on how many lightweight options are fitted (magnesium wheels, polycarbonate rear glazing, carbon-fibre roof, titanium exhaust and so on), while the extreme Aero Pack adds the high-rise rear wing and larger front splitter to further squeeze the GT8's Michelin Pilot Sport Cup 2 tyres into the tarmac. Slot in the key, push, hear the starter spin, then flinch as the V8 bursts into life. Modern Astons like to holler, but the GT8 is on another level – raucous and unapologetic.

However, while the GT12 is all about the fire and brimstone of its incendiary V12, the GT8 is more focused on dynamic prowess. And with its V8 tucked well behind the axle line for a true front-mid-engined layout, it has an immediacy and responsiveness that the GT12 lacks.

Grip is plentiful, but not at the expense of feel. So, while the GT8 feels well within itself at sane speeds, it's always communicative. It works on real roads, too, yielding just enough to work with the road rather than fighting it. With confidence, you learn to trust in the GT8's innate poise, carrying a little more speed into the corner and squeezing the throttle a little earlier and more insistently until each cornering phase melds into one seamless, intoxicating bear hug of lateral g.

The only thing the V8 lacks is torque in the low and mid-ranges. You need to have the tacho needle sweeping beyond 5,000rpm for the car to really hit its stride. Consequently, if you tend to get your kicks between the corners, you'll feel a bit short-changed by the GT8. However, if you delight in the more cerebral satisfaction of cornering, few things are finer than threading a GT8 along a challenging road. Dynamically, it's the brightest and sharpest Vantage there has ever been.

DB11

The DB11 is nothing less than the most important new Aston for more than a decade.

So how does it stack up?

SPECIFICATIONS

Years produced: 2016– **Engine:** V12, 5,204cc, twin-turbo
Max power: 600bhp @ 6,500rpm **Max torque:** 516lb ft @ 1,500–5,000rpm **0–60mph:** 3.7sec
Max speed: 200mph **Price:** £154,900/$214,820 new

T he first new Aston on Andy Palmer's watch; the first since the technical partnership was signed with Mercedes-AMG; the first of a whole new generation of cars; the first turbocharged Aston (if you ignore the one-off Bulldog); and the replacement for the beloved DB9… to say the DB11 has a lot riding on it is an understatement and a half. So, approaching it as an Aston enthusiast, you really want it to be great.

There's lots of the One-77 in the DB11's design: note the way the waist of the car seems to nip in and then the rear arches flare out. The rear of the car in particular is very distinctive, especially the C-pillar, with its integrated Aeroblade intake (the aerodynamics are another facet of the car that takes the DB11 into uncharted waters for Aston). Lift up the beautiful clamshell bonnet and you can see the slatted wheel-arch covers that relieve the high-pressure area around the wheels, the air escaping through a facsimile of the Vulcan's bold side strake.

Inside, if you were to peel away the beautiful brogue leather, you'd now find a Mercedes system underneath much of the switchgear, but any thoughts that this imported technology might demean the ambience of an Aston couldn't be further from the truth. It's a fabulous driving environment.

The chunk of crystal that you used to insert into the dash has been consigned to Aston history; there's now just a large keyless key that you can keep in your pocket. On the dash is a row of five glass buttons, labelled P, R, Start, N and D, and the middle one glows red as you stretch a finger towards it. What it summons is a new, all-alloy, quad-overhead-cam, 5.2-litre twin-turbo V12. Developed by Aston Martin itself, it has 600bhp and 516lb ft of torque and is more powerful than any previous Aston road-car engine, apart from the One-77's naturally aspirated 7.3-litre V12.

It endows the DB11 with monumental and utterly effortless performance – 0–60 in 3.7 seconds is proper supercar territory, as is the 200mph top speed. It's greener than anything we've seen before, too. As well as cylinder deactivation, the new V12 also has stop/start: every time the big V12 spins back into life, it does so with a wonderfully theatrical high-pitched flourish from the starter motor that calls to mind a Lamborghini Aventador.

The attractive, slightly square steering wheel has a button on its right-hand spar that changes the engine and gearbox characteristics – the transmission is the well-proven eight-speed auto with paddleshift – while mirroring it on the left-hand spar is a button for the adaptive suspension. Three modes can be cycled through with each button: GT, Sport and Sport Plus. In GT mode, you can really feel the DB11's relaxed, long-travel suspension breathing with the road through the bigger dips.

On motorways, the DB11 shows its ability to cosset, while covering ground at a tremendous lick. On a quiet Autobahn, frequent forays in the region of 170mph are easy. Just moseying along, covering ground at 100mph, feels good, with the DB11 reassuringly stable, never tense or twitchy. The seats deserve real praise, too. Their shape is slim and the padding doesn't look as if it will overly mollycoddle a posterior, but they definitely work.

Twisting back roads reveal the initially surprising length to the suspension travel. It means the DB11 cushions the lumps and bumps of the road but sacrifices a little bit of instant precision as it moves through that suspension travel as you turn in to the corner. However, the chassis balance is spot-on and, despite a certain remoteness, you still feel in touch with the road. As the tarmac gets wider and smoother, so the DB11 begins to really flow.

There are three ESP options to choose from: On, Off or Track. And, if you can find a suitable hairpin, you'll find the DB11 more than happy to indulge in a bit of sideways fun. The big punch of torque, which feels at its most potent around 4,000rpm, allows you to work the rear wheels. Track mode gives you plenty of slip before it intervenes, and when you throw in surprisingly quick steering and brake-based torque vectoring to help on turn-in, it means this big, 1,770-kg (1.95-ton) car can really be hustled. Down the straights, the DB11 hauls as well as you'd expect, piling on speed in great, thrilling strides. The turbocharged engine isn't the sort of V12 where you feel the need to hang on for the limiter, but under load the raucous exhaust note still sounds unmistakably Aston.

As a taste of the new generation of Astons, the DB11 hits the spot – and, remember, this is the GT in the range. Imagine how exciting the sports cars are going to be…

SPECIFICATIONS

Years produced: 2017– **Engine:** V12, 5,935cc **Max power:** 595bhp @ 7,000rpm
Max torque: 465lb ft @ 5,500rpm **0–60mph:** 3.5sec
Max speed: 201mph **Price:** £199,950/$287,650

2017
Vanquish S

For 2017, the Vanquish was replaced by the Vanquish S, with more power, improved aerodynamics, even sharper responses and a whole lot more intensity

While it had always looked the part as Aston's series-production flagship, the Gaydon-era Vanquish had been something of a slow-burn success. It was a big step forward when it received the eight-speed Touchtronic gearbox, but with the Vantage range becoming faster and increasingly focused – most notably the ferocious V12 Vantage S – and the DB11 combining higher headline power outputs with superior GT credentials, Aston's 'super-GT' was in danger of falling between the cracks.

All that changed with the Vanquish S, unveiled at the end of 2016. A boost in power, improved aerodynamics, revised chassis settings and a host of distinguishing details made for the most comprehensive refresh since the second-generation Vanquish was introduced in 2012.

With a freer-breathing inlet system and revised ECU mapping, the 5.9-litre, naturally aspirated V12 now develops a formidable 595bhp (up from 565bhp). Aston claims 0–60mph in 3.5sec, a couple of tenths quicker than the outgoing car, though the top speed is unchanged at 201mph. Complementing this sharper and stronger delivery, the Touchtronic 3 transmission has had its electronic calibration revised so that it is able to deliver faster gearshifts for a more incisive response.

Meanwhile, damper internals, spring rates and anti-roll bar bushes have all been retuned to give the car a greater sense of control and agility, while preserving the same degree of compliance for a supple ride at low speeds and on less-than-smooth roads via the three-stage ADS (Adaptive Damping System).

Combined, the changes work wonders. With a greater volume of air flowing through the inlet manifolds and into the engine, the way it delivers its power feels more intense, pulling harder all the way to the red line with a greater appetite for revs. The power just builds and builds, accompanied by the most glorious V12 wail, showing what the new generation of turbocharged engines is currently missing. And with the revised suspension giving even tighter control without sacrificing ride quality, the whole car feels more alert. If this is the last hurrah for Aston's epic, naturally aspirated V12 engine, then it's certainly going out on a high.

2017
Vanquish Zagato

The Vanquish is the latest Aston to get the Zagato treatment. Another strictly limited edition, it's an instant collector's piece. Hopefully they won't all be stashed away as investments

SPECIFICATIONS

Years produced: 2017– **Engine:** V12, 5,935cc **Max power:** 595bhp @ 7,000rpm
Max torque: 465lb ft @ 5,500rpm **0–60mph:** 3.5sec
Max speed: 201mph **Price:** £500,000/$735,000

The famous 'Z' of Zagato has come to signify an edgier, more extreme interpretation of Aston Martin design themes, and an enhanced and intensified driving experience. With the 595bhp 5.9-litre V12 engine and brilliantly honed running gear from the Vanquish S, combined with lightweight carbon-fibre bodywork, the Vanquish Zagato is a drivers' Aston from nose to tail. So it's perhaps ironic, and regrettable, that the vast majority are almost certain to be salted away in the dehumidified garages of extremely wealthy collectors and rarely driven in anger.

Dynamically, the new car is inevitably closely related to the Vanquish S. That means an engine that absolutely loves to rev, a spine-tingling soundtrack, instant gear changes summoned at the gentlest tug of the paddleshift, steering that's brimming with feel and precision, and a chassis that somehow blends iron-fisted control with genuine suppleness. If anything, with its short body overhangs and extensive use of one-piece carbon-fibre panels to help reduce weight, the Zagato is even keener to do the driver's bidding than the 'regular' Vanquish. And with its powerful lines and stunning detailing – both inside and out – it's even more of an 'event'.

Visually, the Vanquish Zagato develops many of the themes first explored in the V12 Vantage Zagato. But it also throws in some extra elements: a rear end with a nod to the One-77 supercar and bladed LED rear lights first seen on the Vulcan. Inside, it's just as striking, with aniline (uncoated) leather, quilted in a unique pattern that references the 'Z' motif.

Just 99 cars are being built and, despite a stellar £500,000/$735,000 price tag, all were sold virtually as soon as the model was announced. Aston followed up by announcing an equally limited-edition open-top Volante version soon after. Again, just 99 Volantes are to be built, at a price of around £575,000/$820,000. Apparently, at least one was sold to a customer who already had an order for the coupé version…

2019

Valkyrie

The ultimate supercar, designed by an F1 genius and wearing the Aston Martin wings…

Here's what's known so far about the extraordinary Valkyrie

SPECIFICATIONS

Projected build: 2019– **Engine:** V12, 6.5 litres, with KERS **Max power:** c.1,000bhp
Max torque: n/a **0–60mph:** sub3.0sec
Max speed: 200mph+ **Price:** £2–3 million/$2.48–3.73 million new

T o redefine the limits of road car performance. That's the extraordinarily bold mission statement for the Valkyrie. And it would be tempting to dismiss it as hyperbole, were it not for the fact that this remarkable, convention-challenging hypercar is the brainchild of Adrian Newey. As the world's most successful – and therefore revered – designer of Grand Prix racing cars, Newey's name carries unique gravitas in the world of fast cars.

So, what do we know about the Valkyrie so far? That it will have a brand-new, 6.5-litre, naturally aspirated engine, designed and built by Cosworth. That it will feature a 'lightweight hybrid battery system', which suggests some sort of F1-style Kinetic Energy Recovery System (KERS) style

arrangement. That its aerodynamics will be the most advanced ever seen in a roadgoing supercar. And that every single one is already sold, long before deliveries are due to start in 2019.

The Valkyrie is very much Newey's car. This is his vision of the ultimate supercar, much as the McLaren F1 was for fellow genius race-car designer Gordon Murray. The coup for Aston Martin and, therefore, boss Andy Palmer is that Newey's car will be an Aston, both through choice – Newey is a fan of the brand and has owned Astons prior to this project – and through a long-standing relationship between Palmer and Red Bull that goes back to Palmer's time at Nissan and Infiniti.

What's in it for Red Bull? Well, apart from being associated with one of the coolest, most well-known and – in

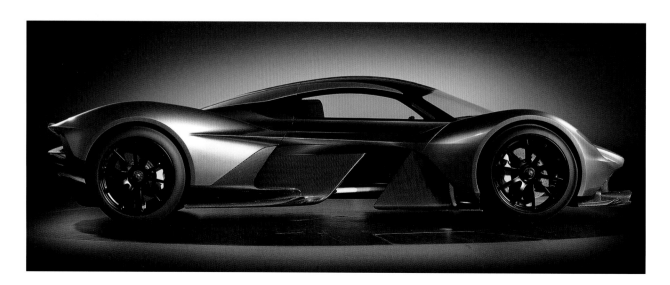

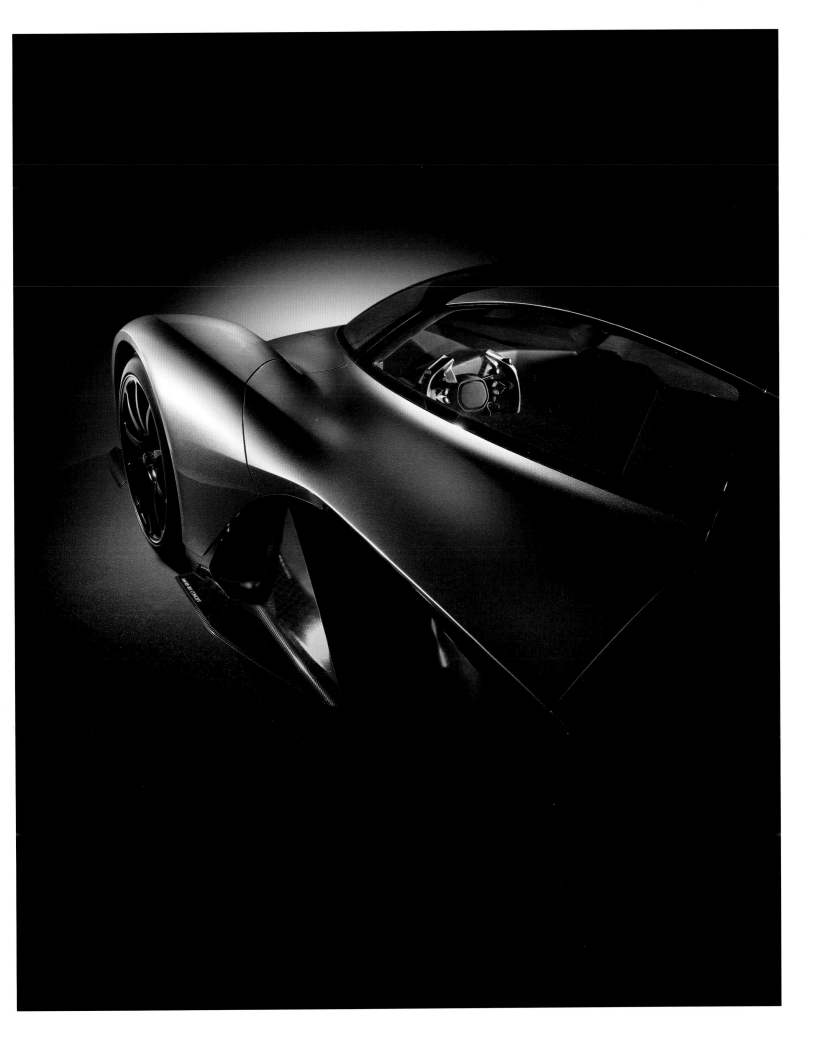

recent times – most dynamic car companies on the planet, the Valkyrie is the perfect showcase for the race team's engineering consultancy offshoot, Red Bull Advanced Technologies.

So, what about the car? Well, as you'd expect, it borrows heavily from Newey's unrivalled experience in creating ultra-fast race cars, but also from his love of racing historic cars, such as his Ford GT40. This said, he insists the Valkyrie will be no race-track refugee. According to Newey and his collaborator on the project, Aston design director Marek Reichman, it accommodates two full-size male occupants, though there's no room for luggage. At 190cm (6¼ft) wide, it's narrower than the current breed of hypercar. Likewise, its 400cm (13ft) length makes it comfortably shorter than a Cayman-sized sports car and it stands a little over a metre (39in) high, lower even than the legendary GT40.

The materials that will be used in its construction are suitably exotic. Indeed, there is no steel component anywhere. Carbon fibre will be used extensively, in thicknesses dictated by F1 standards of design and construction for immense strength and rigidity, but only where it's needed.

It's all in aid of achieving a power-to-weight ratio of 1:1 – that's to say, 1bhp for every 1kg (2¼lb) of weight. No one is saying what the weight will be or, indeed, the power output of the still-secret engine, but the smart money is on a car weighing as close to 1,000kg (1.1 tons) as is possible, meaning the car will need as close to 1,000bhp as possible.

The bulk of this will come from a high-revving, naturally aspirated, 6.5-litre V12 engine developed by Cosworth. The new unit is described by Aston as 'the ultimate road-legal internal combustion engine'. It will be mated to a similarly bespoke seven-speed paddle-shift transmission, designed and manufactured by Ricardo, to Red Bull Advanced Technologies' specification. And it will be supplemented by a KERS, much like that developed for recent F1 cars, which will add around 100bhp and a very useful slug of torque to boost the low- and mid-range acceleration.

The powertrain will be without compromise, as Newey explained at the concept's unveiling in summer 2016: 'It's a bespoke V12, a start-from-scratch engine. It'll be high-revving with a very high specific output per litre.'

The shape of the body is truly extraordinary, and the really dramatic stuff sits underneath the car: vast, canyon-sized venturi tunnels channelling air either side of the teardrop-shaped cockpit and feeding a gargantuan rear diffuser. The enormously aggressive underbody will generate huge levels of downforce, so much, in fact, that the suspension system is expected to feature active technology to combat the vertical loadings and enable a combination of low-speed pliancy and high-speed control.

There is also the prospect of a track-only version (Aston has said there will be 150 road cars and 25 track cars) that will be able to lap a circuit such as Silverstone at a similar pace to today's LMP1 Le Mans prototypes.

How much? Aston Martin says somewhere between £2 million/$2.5 million and £3 million/$3.7 million. Deliveries are due to start in 2019, but before then a vast amount of work remains to be done. It's a hugely ambitious project for any road-car brand – Aston included – but one that's firmly within the scope of a front-running F1 team. The result promises to be mind-blowing.

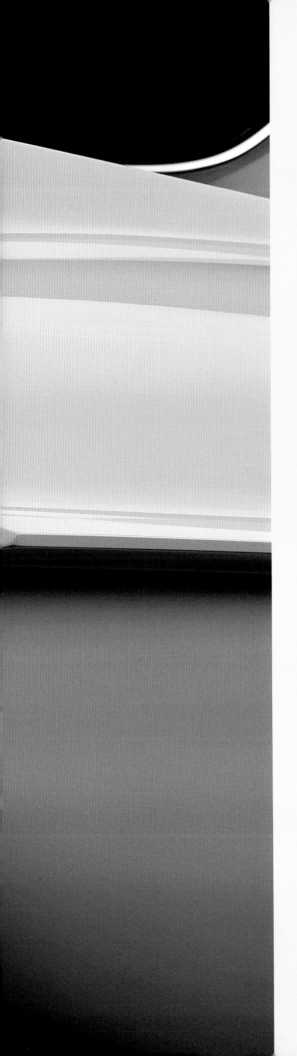

BESPOKE ASTONS

**Every Aston Martin is special,
but some are more special than others**

A ston Martin Rapide not quite commodious enough for you? How about an estate version? DB4 GT just not quite fabulous enough? Then what you need is a one-off coach-built version by Italian styling house Bertone.

For the mega-rich enthusiast, the cars in the showroom have often been just the starting point for their flights of fancy. For those with deep pockets and a yearning to drive something truly exceptional, regular bodywork and interiors can always be replaced with something completely bespoke.

Over the years, a number of famous coach-builders – and Aston Martin itself – have built a series of intriguing and sometimes outlandish variations on familiar Aston themes.

In the 1950s, when coach-building was still widespread, it was not unusual to take a rolling chassis to an Italian *carrozzeria* (body shop) for a snazzy new set of clothes. The Aston Martin DB2/4 was a particular favourite for the treatment, the great Italian styling houses of the day always keen to dress the current Aston rolling chassis with the latest fashions in aluminium.

One of the most striking results was the DB2/4 Supersonic by esteemed *carrozzeria* Ghia, revealed at the 1956 Turin motor show. Inspired by the age of jet transport, the Supersonic was designed to capture the themes of the age – speed, power and progress – in its taut, streamlined forms, delicate use of brightwork and vestigial tail fins.

Another variation on the same chassis was the Vignale-bodied DB2/4 with its striking wraparound rear screen, built in 1954 for the King of Belgium. And when Carrozzeria Touring produced its DB2/4 Spyder in 1956, the Aston management were so impressed that they gave Touring the job of styling the next full production model – the car we now know as the DB4.

Jet-age Aston: DB2/4 Supersonic detail

DB2/4 Supersonic was created by Ghia in 1956

Bertone, too, produced a Spyder version of the DB2/4, but its best-known creation around Aston underpinnings is the 1961 DB4 GT Jet. Built on the rolling chassis and fabulous twin-plug engine of the DB4 GT road-racer, the Jet was the work of a young Giorgetto Giugiaro, who had recently joined Bertone and would, of course, go on to design some of the world's best-known cars. As with many of these bespoke vehicles, just one example was ever built. Today it's one of the most valuable Astons of all – in 2013 it sold for £3,249,500/$4,084,612 at auction.

Estates are a whole sub-genre of bespoke Astons. It was David Brown himself who commissioned the first Aston Martin 'shooting brake' – the nomenclature no doubt chosen to reflect his private enthusiasms as a hunting, shooting, fishing sort of chap. Almost all subsequent models have followed the same naming convention – somehow 'Aston Martin estate' doesn't have quite the same ring.

While the regular DB5 was very much to Brown's liking, it was a bit of a squeeze when he needed to carry polo equipment, hunting gear and/or dogs. So, in 1964, he asked the factory to create a DB5 shooting brake for his personal use. Only problem was, friends and business associates decided they wanted one, too. The factory couldn't have coped with building a third body style alongside the saloon and convertible DB5, not since demand had been fuelled by a certain secret agent's endorsement. So Brown did a deal with Harold Radford (Coachbuilders) Ltd. The conversion affected everything from the windscreen backwards, and the price was 50 per cent more than the saloon. Hardly surprising, then, that there were just 12 of them. Radford later built a shooting brake version of the DB6, of which just six were built.

DB2/4 also formed the basis for this Spyder by Touring

214

Below and left: sublime DB4 GT Jet by Bertone

DB2/4 Vignale was created for Belgian royalty

Brown's Radford-bodied DB5 shooting brake not only became a personal favourite of the boss, but also inspired other wealthy Aston Martin enthusiasts to commission their own over the years, with, it has to be said, varying degrees of aesthetic success. All, however, offer an enticing combination of pace and space, and – because they were invariably built in tiny numbers due to the eye-watering cost of conversion – the added appeal of something highly individual and, in some cases, unique.

Among those who followed DB's lead was racing driver Innes Ireland. No doubt having cast envious eyes over DB's DB5 wagon, in 1969 he had his DB6 converted to a shooting brake by F L M Panelcraft Ltd, a Kings Cross-based coach-builder. The same company later converted a DBS for a Scottish laird with a love of angling and a need to carry rods, tackle and salmon – a unique feature was a full-length roof rack to carry his rods.

Some Astons have definitely been more conducive to the shooting brake treatment than others. Swiss engineering company and Aston Martin dealer Roos has built a number of examples over the years, including estate versions of the William Towns Lagonda wedge and the 1990s Virage and supercharged Vantage. The latter was achieved with full factory co-operation. Built over two years, the conversion involved a new roof, chassis strengthening and 1,800 hours of craftsmanship. Commendably, the end result weighed only 60kg (132lb) more than the donor car and was claimed to be 'the fastest and strongest estate car in the world'. With its 0–60mph time of 3.9 seconds, we must assume the German owner was suitably satisfied.

Several coachbuilders built DB5 and DB6 estates; this one was by Radford

This unique DBS shooting brake was built for a Scottish laird

Even the Lagonda got the estate treatment, here by Kielstra

217

Vanquish Roadster by Zagato looked producton-ready

DB9 and DBS-based Zagatos marked the Aston Centenary

Aston itself built this Lagonda-badged Virage-based estate

Jet 2+2 of 2013 was based on the Rapide

In the 1990s, Aston Martin itself built a number of special variations on the Virage theme, including a three-door shooting brake and a five-door version that was badged as a Lagonda. There was also a series of special-bodied coupés, loosely inspired by the classic DB4 GT Zagato and built for one particularly wealthy Far Eastern client, who ordered six at a time on condition that no one else could have one. It's not exaggerating to say that the building of these cars helped to keep the Newport Pagnell operation going through some distinctly sticky times.

The independent styling houses haven't been averse to taking inspiration from their own back catalogues. In 2004, Bertone unveiled Jet 2, a concept car created in homage to the original 1960s DB4 GT-based Bertone Jet and based on the bonded aluminium and carbon-fibre chassis of a pre-production V12 Vanquish, lengthened by 210mm (8¼in). Only the basic structure, mechanicals and windscreen were retained from the donor car; all the body panels and most of the interior were bespoke. The car, which has remained a one-off and the personal property of Lilli Bertone, widow of the company founder, resurfaced at the Geneva motor show in 2013, revamped with extra rear space.

The same show saw the debut of another Bertone-penned Aston one-off, the Rapide-based Jet 2+2, specially built for a British businessman. So favourable was the reception for the stretched and reshaped Rapide that Aston Martin was rumoured to be in discussions with Bertone about building a limited run, but nothing materialized.

AML had, of course, continued to collaborate occasionally with Zagato, giving rise to special-bodied versions of the DB7 and V12 Vantage, though these were usually for runs of around 100 cars each. For 2013, Aston Martin's centenary year, Zagato announced three far rarer Aston-based cars: a DB9 Spyder, DBS Coupé and Virage Shooting Brake. Each was a pure one-off, created for a wealthy enthusiast.

Above and right: GT12 Roadster by Aston's Q division

Aston Martin's own birthday present to itself was the CC100 speedster. Originally intended as a one-off, a second example was later built after another valued customer asked especially nicely.

The CC100 gave Aston a real taste for building bespoke cars, and in recent years it has promoted its 'Q by Aston Martin' division, offering the chance for customers not only to specify special colours and trim, but even to commission whole-car design and engineering projects. A recent example was the one-off Roadster version of the ferocious Vantage GT12 road-racer, unveiled in 2016. The expansion of Q means we can look forward to more 'official' Aston one-offs in the future.

But Aston Martin and favoured styling houses like Zagato by no means have a monopoly on producing such exotic creations. One of the most spectacular bespoke Astons of recent times is the Boniolo V12 Vanquish EG Shooting Brake. Designed by Francesco Boniolo, who heads a design house of the same name, and constructed by Quality Cars of Vigonza, Italy, this Vanquish-based shooting brake was commissioned by an anonymous customer who lent his initials to the car. It features a lengthened chassis that allowed the fitment of 'suicide' rear doors to give better access to the more generous rear seats. The hatchback coachwork is finished in traditional British Racing Green and the interior covered in lobster-coloured leather by Pineider, with bamboo wood cappings to the doors and dash. Now that's bespoke!

Striking Boniolo-designed Vanquish Shooting Brake

Index

An Hachette UK Company
www.hachette.co.uk

First published in Great Britain in 2017 by Mitchell Beazley, a division of
Octopus Publishing Group Ltd
Carmelite House
50 Victoria Embankment
London EC4Y 0DZ
www.octopusbooks.co.uk
www.octopusbooksusa.com

Distributed in the US by
Hachette Book Group
1290 Avenue of the Americas
4th and 5th Floors
New York, NY 10020

Distributed in Canada by
Canadian Manda Group
664 Annette St.
Toronto, Ontario, Canada M6S 2C8

ISBN 978-1-78472-269-2

A CIP catalogue record for this book is available from the British Library.

Printed and bound in the UK

10 9 8 7 6 5 4 3 2

Commissioning Editor: Joe Cottington
Senior Editor: Pauline Bache
Copyeditor: Helen Ridge
Consultant on US prices: Marc Noordeloos
Design Manager: Jack Storey
Designer: Jeremy Tilston
Senior Production Controller: Allison Gonsalves
Text compiled by Peter Tomalin

Picture acknowledgements
Alamy Stock Photo National Motor Museum/Heritage Image Partnership Ltd. 122 above. **Aston Martin Heritage Trust** 12 right, 14 below, 15 above right, 26 right, 27 above left, 27 below right, 86 left, 86 right, 87 below left, 87 above right, 121 above, 123. **Bonhams** 15 below right. **Courtesy of Aston Martin** 118, 125, 126 above left, 126 below left, 126 above, 126 below, 130, 131 above, 131 centre, 131 below, 132, 133 above, 133 below left, 133 below right. **REX Shutterstock** LAT Photographic 120 below, 122 below.

Octane Media photographer acknowledgements
Tim Andrew 56–7, 60–1, 70–1, 81, 94–5, 218 (main image); **Aston Martin** 118, 126–7, 130–3, 178–81, 206–7, 220–1; **Michael Baillie** 28–9; Nick Dimbleby 148–51; **Max Earey** 8–9, 199–203; **Jacob Ebrey** 98–9, 104–5; **Dominic Fraser** 182–3; **Gus Gregory** 34–5, 46–7, 62–5, 90–1, 110–1, 114–5, 134–7, 162–3, 176–7; **Matthew Howell** 4–5, 16–7, 22, 32–3, 38–45, 52–5, 66–9, 76, 78, 82–3, 88–9, 154–5, 168–75, 188–9, 204–5, 218 (main image); **Justin Leighton** 72–3; **James Lipman** 48–51, 58–9, 92–3, 100–3, 138–41, 158–61, 184–5; **Charlie Magee** 74–5, 208–11; **Andy Morgan** 18–21, 106–9, 144–7, 152–3, 194–7; **Kenny P** 142–3; **Aston Parrott** 190–3; **Dean Smith** 112–3, 116–7, 164–7, 186–7; **Alex Tapley** 30–1; **Tim Wallace** 36–7; **John Wycherley** 96